More Light
Masonic Enlightenment Series

Edited by Michael R. Poll

More Light

A Cornerstone Book
Published by Cornerstone Book Publishers
Copyright © 2008 by Michael R. Poll

Cover image, *A Labor of Love* by Sam Brown, available as a print at:
www.lostword.com

Published by Cornerstone Book Publishers
New Orleans, LA
USA

First Cornerstone Edition - 2008

www.cornerstonepublishers.com

ISBN: 1-934935-36-0
ISBN 13: 978-1-934935-36-1

MADE IN THE USA

Table of Contents

More Light

The Square
Joseph Fort Newton

The Holy Bible lies open upon the Altar of Masonry, and upon the bible lie the Square and Compasses. They are the three Great Lights of the Lodge, at once its Divine warrant and its chief working tools. They are symbols of Revelation, Righteousness, and Redemption, teaching us that by walking in the light of Truth and obeying the law of Right, the Divine in man wins victory over the earthly. How to live is the one important matter, and he will seek far without finding a wiser way than that shown us by the Great Lights of the Lodge.

The Square and Compasses are the oldest, the simplest, and the most universal symbols of Masonry. All the world over, whether as a sign on a building, or a badge worn by a Brother, even the profane know them to be emblems of our ancient Craft. Some Years ago, when a business firm tried to adopt the Square and Compasses as a trademark, the Patent Office refused permission, on the ground, as the decision said, that "there can be no doubt that this device, so commonly worn and employed by Masons, has an established mystic significance, universally recognized as existing; whether comprehended by all or not, is not material to this issue." They belong to such, alike by the associations of history and the tongue of common report.

Nearly everywhere in our Ritual, as in the public mind, the Square and Compasses are seen together. If not interlocked, they are seldom far apart, and the one suggests the other. And that is as it should be, because the things they symbolize are interwoven. In the old days when the earth was thought to be flat and square, the Square was an emblem of the earth, and later, of the earthly element, as the sky is an arc or a circle, the implement which describes a Circle became the symbol of the heavenly, or sky spirit in man. Thus the tools of the builder became the emblems of the thoughts of the thinker; and nothing in Masonry is more impressive than the slow elevation of the Compasses above the Square in the progress of the degrees. The whole meaning and task of life is there, for such as have eyes to see.

Let us separate the Square from the Compasses and study it alone, the better to see sits further meaning and use. There is no need to say that the Square we have in mind is not a Cube, which has four equal sides and angles, deemed by the Greeks a figure of perfection. Nor is it the square of the carpenter, one leg of which is longer than the other, with inches marked for measuring. It is a small, plain Square, unmarked and with legs of equal length, a simple try-square used for testing the accuracy of angles, and the precision with which stones are cut. Since the try-square was used to prove that angles were right, it naturally became an emblem of accuracy, integrity, rightness. As stones are cut to fit into a building, so our acts and thoughts are built together into a structure of Character, badly or firmly, and must be tested by a moral standard of which the simple try-square is a symbol.

So, Among Speculative Masons, the tiny try-square has always been a symbol of mortality, of the basic rightness which must be the test of every act and the foundation of character and society. From the beginning of the Revival in 1717 this was made plain in the teaching of Masonry, by the fact that the Holy bible was placed upon the Altar, along with the Square and Compasses. In one of the earliest catechisms of the Craft, dated 1725, the question is asked: "How many make a lodge?" The answer is specific and unmistakable: "God and the square, with five or seven right or perfect Masons." God and the Square, Religion and Morality, must be present in every lodge as its ruling Lights, or it fails of being a just and truly constituted lodge. In all lands, in all rites where Masonry is true to itself, the Square is a symbol of righteousness, and is applied in the light of faith in God.

God and the Square: it is necessary to keep the two together in our day, because the tendency of the time is to separate them. The idea in vogue today is that morality is enough, and that faith in God if there be a God may or may not be important. Some very able men of the Craft insist that we make the teaching of Masonry too religious Whereas, as all history shows, if faith in God grows dim, morality becomes a mere custom, if not a cobweb, to be thrown off lightly. It is not rooted in reality, and so lacks authority and sanction. Such an idea, such a spirit, so widespread in our time, and finding so many able and plausible advocates strikes at the foundations, not only of Masonry, but of all ordered and advancing social life. Once let men come to think that morality is a human invention, and not a part of the order of the world, and the moral law will lose both its meaning and its power. Far wiser was the old book entitled ALL IN ALL AND

THE SAME FOREVER, by John Advise, and dated 1607, though written by a non-Mason, when it read the reality and nature of God in this manner: "Yet I this form of formless Deity drew by the Square and Compasses of our Creed." For, inevitable, a society without standards will be a society without stability, and it will one day go down. Not only nations, but whole civilizations have perished in the past, for lack of righteousness. History speaks plainly in this matter, and we dare not disregard it. Hence the importance attached to the Square or Virtue, and the reason why Masons call it the great symbol of their Craft. It is a symbol of that moral law upon which human life must rest if it is to stand. A man may build a house in any way he likes, but if he expects it to stand and be his home, he must adjust his structure to the laws and forces that rule in the material realm. Just so, unless we live in obedience to the moral laws which God has written in the order of things, our lives will fall and end in wreck. When a young man forgets the simple Law of the Square, it does not need a prophet to foresee what the result will be. It is like a problem in geometry.

Such has been the meaning of the Square as far back as we can go. Long before our era we find the Square teaching the same lesson which it teaches us today. In one of the old books of China, called THE GREAT LEARNING, which has been dated in the fifth century before Christ, we read that a man should not do unto others what he would not have then do unto him; and the writer adds, "This is called the principle of acting of the square." There it is recorded long, long ago. The greatest philosopher has found nothing more profound, and the oldest man in his ripe wisdom has learned nothing more true. Even Jesus only altered it from the negative to the positive form in His Golden Rule. So, everywhere, in our Craft and outside, the Square has taught its simple truth which does not grow old. The Deputy Provincial Grand Master of North and East Yorkshire recovered a very curious relic, in the form of an old brass Square found under the foundation of an ancient bridge near Limerick, in 1830. On it was inscribed the date, 1517, and the following words:

> "Strive to live with love and care
> Upon the Level, by the Square."

How simple and beautiful it is, revealing the oldest wisdom man has learned and the very genius of our Craft. In fact and truth, the Square rules the Mason as well as the lodge in which he labors. As soon as he enters a lodge, the candidate walks with square steps round the square pavement of a rectangular lodge. All during the ceremony his attitude keeps ;him in mind of the same symbol, as if to fashion his life after its form. When he is brought to light, he beholds the Square upon the Altar, and at the same time sees that it is worn by the Master of the lodge, as the emblem of his office. In the north east corner he is shown the perfect Ashlar, and told that it the type of a finished Mason, who must be a Square-man in thought and conduct, in word and act. With every art of emphasis the Ritual writes this lesson in our hearts, and if we forget this first truth the Lost Word will remain forever lost.

For Masonry is not simple a Ritual; it is a way of living. It offers us a plan, a method, a faith by which we may build our days and years into a character so strong and true that nothing, not even death, can destroy it. Each of us has in his own heart a little try-square called Conscience, by which to test each thought and deed and word, whether it be true or false. By as much as a man honestly applies that test in his own heart, and in his relations with his fellows, by so much will his life be happy, stable, and true. Long ago the question was asked and answered: "Lord, who shall abide in thy tabernacle? He that walketh uprightly, and worketh righteousness, and speaketh the truth in his heart." It is the first obligation of a Mason to be on the Square, in all his duties and dealing with his fellow men, and if he fails there he cannot win anywhere. Let one of our poets sum it all up:

> *It Matters not whate'er your lot*
> *or what your task may be*
> *One duty there remains for you,*
> *One duty stands for me.*
> *Be you a doctor skilled and wise,*
> *Or do your work for Wage,*
> *A laborer upon the street,*
> *An artist on the stage;*
> *One glory still awaits for you.*
> *One honor that is fair,*
> *To have men say as you pass by:*
> *"That Fellow's on the square."*
> *Ah, here's a phrase that stands for much,*

Tis good old English, too;
It means that men have confidence
In everything you do.
It means that what you have you've earned,
And that you've done your best
And when you go to sleep at night
Untroubled you may rest.
It means that conscience is your guide,
And honor is your care;
There is no greater praise than this:
"That fellow's on the square."
And when I die I would not wish
A lengthy epitaph;
I do not want a headstone large,
Carved with fulsome chaff.
Pick out no single deed of mine,
If such a deed there be,
To 'grave upon my monument,
For those who come to see.
Just this one phrase of all I choose,
To show my life was fair:
"Here sleepeth now a fellow who
Was always on the square."

Mythology and Masonry

R.J. Meekren

The great difficulty in undertaking to write on a Masonic topic is that one never knows where to begin. I had it in mind to discuss the relationship of the Ancient Mysteries and primitive initiations to our Speculative Masonry, what use could be properly made of them in seeking light upon our own origins: and there was a strong temptation to begin with a disquisition upon symbolism, and the evolution of meaning in the use of traditional symbols. But had that been undertaken it would doubtless have involved a preliminary discussion of something else. And after all it behooves a Mason to keep himself within due bounds, even when writing articles for Masonic magazines! (Verbum sat sapienti!)

The earlier generation of Masonic students, perhaps even as far back as Dr. Stukely, were much impressed by the resemblances between Freemasonry and what they knew of the Ancient Mysteries. Dr. Oliver is a prominent case in point. Yet he is only one among many and is only typical of what, till comparatively recently, was not only the prevailing but practically the only school of Masonic scholarship, and one that even today, in spite of a general reaction to the other extreme, has exponents who must be treated seriously and with respect, however one may object to their arguments or disagree with their conclusions.

The earlier scholars were handicapped by mistaken ideas of what the Mysteries of Greece, Egypt and other Mediterranean peoples really were. There seems indeed to be the same ignorance in many quarters today, but while it was then unavoidable, now it is hardly excusable. It will not be necessary to set-out in any detail for readers of THE BUILDER this type of speculation. All those who read at all about Masonic subjects must have come across it ad libitum if not ad nauseam. The Mysteries were taken to be occult or mystical schools of transcontinental philosophy. The myths of Osiris, Admis, Baldur and the like were treated as consciously devised allegories, and the whole was interpreted by a literal reference to the Old Testament. The myths in their literary forms, and the notices of the Mysteries in the better known classics, were mingled together, all being supposed to be but variants of one original, that is to say of Freemasonry, which was originated by Solomon, or Moses, or Enoch, or even Adam. What was found in one place was freely transferred to fill up a gap elsewhere without any warrant in fact or original authority and the result described in purely Masonic terminology.

The story of Osiris has perhaps been the favorite one of such writers, possibly because it is known in such great detail. And this oft-repeated tale really has many resemblances to certain legends known to most Masons which it would be needless here to point out. But these are not all above suspicion. It is even possible that Masonic legend has been modified under the influence of Osirian myth. In the oldest versions of the former there is no mention of the Acacia, which figures so curiously in the account of the last Osiris, but Cassia definitely takes its place. It would have been very easy for learned brethren, full of the idea of a Masonry originating at the building of the Temple at Jerusalem or in the Wilderness of Sinai, or the Garden of Eden, to assume that "Cassia" was an ignorant corruption of "Acacia". One may note Mackey's scorn for the humble "Cassia" in his Encyclopedia. It would have been so easy to make the change - so easy indeed as to arouse our suspicions. In any case the Osiris myth in the form we have it in Herodotus and other Greek authors, the form used for comparison, is a very late one. That is, it was produced, or put together, or at least set down, in the Hellenistic age, in an atmosphere not essentially different from that of today, under the influence of eclectic learning and archaeological pedantry.

THE MYSTERIES TAUGHT NO OCCULT SECRETS

These myths, in their literary forms at least, had nothing much to do with the Mysteries. They would have to be used with the same caution and discrimination that would be needed if one were to reconstruct the Masonic ritual from articles and notes on the subject in Masonic periodicals. On the other hand, there was no deep mystical teaching propagated by the Mysteries nor did they possess any occult secrets. Though it was very natural that those making the first researches into the subject in modern times should have fancied that some transcendent doctrine, some wonderful teaching that the common herd was not able to receive, was hidden by the veil of secrecy. In late classical references there are undoubted hints to this effect, but whatever there was of that had been read into the Mysteries by just such earnest-minded initiates as produce the fine spun webs of symbolism in Masonry today, the sort of thing with which we are all familiar.

Originally and primitively the chief content of these secret religious institutions was not a common body of knowledge but a common emotion. There were instructions without doubt, but they would be of a simple straightforward type - rules of conduct and morality, of special tabus, of ritual requirements, very similar, one must suppose, mutatis mutandis, to the contents of the familiar charges of a Freemason.

Since the advent of the scientific and critical method in studying the problems of comparative religion a new field has been opened to the zealous Masonic symbolist. It is very easy to range through collected accounts of savage customs and tribal initiations to find analogies to Freemasonry. It has been discovered that in Australia the candidates (that is, the boys who are being "made men") are hoodwinked (they are not, as a matter of fact, completely blindfolded, but generally merely instructed to keep their eyes on the ground), that they receive an apron (I simply do not know what this refers to; in some other countries and among other races girdles or loin clothes are worn after initiation) and pass through a succession of degrees (which seems to refer to the fact that after the initiation the youth only comes by a gradual process to full rights in the tribe) and other like correspondences. This sort of thing is utterly misleading, not to say absurd. The real connection, if any exist, would not be in any such trifling and obvious matter, details that seem rather inherent in the character of the ceremonies and the nature of the human mind than marks of relationship. One parallel has been overlooked by writers of this class. Most savages mark or mutilate the body in their initiatory rites; in Australia, circumcision and the knocking out of teeth; elsewhere tattooing and cutting marks on back or breast are in vogue. A hundred years ago it was popularly believed that the Freemason was branded - though upon what part of his person was not known. Perhaps it is better not to proceed too far on this line of research, though there are legends of red-hot pokers or gridirons on which the victim had to sit! But let this remain, as it is, wrapped in mystery!

MASONIC SIGNS AMONG SAVAGES

The comparative method has been of great value in many fields of investigation. It has been a key to unlock unsuspected treasures of relationships, and has led to the comprehension and elucidation of many puzzles. But the kind of procedure spoken of above only resembles the comparative method in the most superficial manner. By the one all the facts available are brought together and compared without preconception; in the other an artificial whole is built up out of isolated facts to fit a plausible hypothesis - somewhat like those skeletons of mermaids fashioned by the wily Oriental out of selected bones of monkeys and fishes. There is no value, for instance, in calling the oldest "medicine" man present at the "Borah" ceremonies a "Worshipful Master" - or the two next senior to him "Wardens". There is absolutely no parallel. Any group, society or institution tends to produce rulers or leaders - such analogies prove altogether too much. Or again, to make the statement, so often repeated, that various people and tribes in different parts of the world are acquainted with and use the Masonic signs is very unsafe to say the least. In the first place such statements are too general to be wholly reliable. Where definite cases are adduced the evidence is usually third or fourth hand, and in any case the original signs of Freemasonry seem to have been conventionalized forms of very natural and commonly used gestures, the defining feature being largely in a convention which is very familiar to every "York" Rite Mason at least. Under such circumstances there is nothing more easy than to make such assertions, and nothing much harder than to prove them. There is one sign, however, that appears to have been used at the emergence of Freemasonry into the historic period - that is, 1717 or thereabouts - which is now apparently obsolete in the Symbolic Degrees. This does seem to have been employed in divers times and places - such as in Ancient Egypt, Assyria, India, South America - as a significant gesture. Often represented as being made by divine personages. But what its meaning was is not clear, nor even if it meant anything like the same thing in the different places where it appears. And here again it may be merely a coincidence that it resembles a supposed Masonic sign. For this latter may have really been no more than the conventional form of a gesture most natural to human kind under the stress of certain emotions.

What then is the use of seeking for analogies to Freemasonry in the myths and folklore of ancient and alien peoples? The fault is not with the general method, but with the uncritical way in which it has too often been carried out. The idea is sound enough in itself. As a matter of fact, from the objective point of view, Freemasonry is a traditional survival. To the anthropologist it is as instructive as a living dinosaur would be to a biologist. The myth-making faculty has been supposed to be quite dead and utterly foreign to the minds of civilized men - whereas it is not. It has been, and is, flourishing like the Psalmist's "green bay tree" right in our midst. In Masonry we have a ritual whose origin is simply swathed in layers of myth, and yet still exerts a potent influence over the minds of those who come in real touch with it. Aside from the ritual itself there are all kinds of myths about it, and these have simply grown - they have not been invented by any one man - though it must be admitted that writers like Oliver, Morris et al did much to tend and water a plant that really needs very little cultivation to grow and spread. Just as a minor instance: There was recently published in a Masonic periodical of repute a detailed exposition of a part of the last chapter of Ecclesiastes. When it came to the metaphor of the "silver cord" a purely mythical Oriental custom was adduced, to-wit, that it was usual to hang lamps by silver cords. Whatever the actual figure was in the mind of "the Preacher," and it is very probable it was a very definite and concrete one, it is impossible to believe it was anything so inane as this. This invention of reasons is exactly on a par with mammoth bones being explained as Jonah's whale, or that the cross bill bird got its beak twisted by pecking at the nails that fastened our Lord to the cross.

It is now generally known that the Mysteries, properly so called, had their origin in a far more primitive, not to say savage, state of society than that of the highly civilized Greeks or Romans; that they were in fact survivals. Institutions similar to their hypothetical originals are to be found among most of the primitive peoples of the world, and they there appear a "totem ceremonies", tribal initiations, and the like. Now one feature that all these have in common is the working of magic. The bear or other totem is wakened in the spring by magical dances. The corn is ceremonially planted, the emu is imitated that it may increase, the sun is given new power by midsummer bonfires, or fiery wheels, or burning arrows. And here it may be noted that the primary reason for the secrecy which veils these things is quite practical. It is that they are dangerous. Originally they are open secrets, but it does not do to talk about them except at the proper time, which in the end comes to this that the only place to learn them is at the inaction of the rites themselves and so eventually they are mysteries to all but the initiated. For the spoken word is of great magical power, and of all words the name is the most powerful. To speak of the devil is to raise him. It may be here that we have a clue to the original meaning of the Lost Word.

WHEN DID IT ORIGINATE?

Now where the ultimate origin of all this is to be looked for would be difficult to say. There are strange hints that it may be as far back as the Cro-Magnon cave artists, or even the earlier Aurignacian flint workers, but for our present purpose (and in the present space) it is fortunately as unnecessary as it is impossible to go into this. But it must, however, be emphasized that this magical outlook is an essential element in all the activities of primitive man, as much so apparently in the interglacial periods in Europe as it is today in Africa and Australia. When a savage wants to do anything he is as practical about it from his own point of view as we are, though he mingles with his material means purely magical rites and incantations. In a higher stage the two sides begin to be differentiated and the magic becomes venerable and awful and tends to be worked only occasionally, and by special persons. But to the primitive mind the two things have never been differentiated or distinguished, and magic is an affair of everyday life. The savage still mixes the expression of his desire or need in word and gesture with his action to attain the end in view. To him the former is as necessary as the latter (to some extent it may be so psychologically) and the root of all magic is the expression, by symbol, by song (that is, incantation), by dramatic dance of the individual and, still more, of the collective wish. In the tribal initiations the boys are taught certain things that it is supposed proper that men should know. And this to us seems the real practical purpose of the institution. To the savage this aspect is largely, if not entirely, incidental. The real object in his mind is to magically enable the boy - hitherto an indeterminate "woman-thing" - to become a man, to endue him with the powers a man must have, to separate him entirely from the influence of women and the things of his childhood.

Now as culture advances and tribes amalgamate into races and nations, and religion develops and emerges from undifferentiated magic - one cannot here go into the question of the origin of religion - all kinds of things may happen. The final result may vary all the way from the awful secrets of the initiation becoming the games of children to, on the other hand, the ceremonies becoming the property of a select and organized society. And where this last has occurred we get such secret organizations as flourish in parts of Africa and elsewhere. Or else we get such institutions as the Mysteries, of Demeter and Kore in Eleusis, of Dionysus in Thrace, of Zeus in Crete. In many cases they become, quite naturally, organizations of men of a certain class or occupation. The earliest and most universal of these last is perhaps that of magicians, medicine men, or shamans. Instances of these are to be found almost everywhere - in New Guinea, West Africa, South America, ancient Egypt and Babylonia. Of the last part of the ritual is still extant on inscribed clay tablets. But though such ceremonies were perhaps more likely to become the machine and trades union of professional magicians, the undifferentiated magic of primitive man could quite easily find other lines of development and survival. As man, after having been a hunter, entered the pastoral stage magic ceremonies were required to increase his flocks and herds, and as he became a tiller of the soil magic was again necessary to secure the fertility of his fields and to ensure the sun and rain necessary to his crops and to ward off destructive tempests. The far-famed rites of Eleusis were originally purely of this character. That their agricultural forms were later developed into a bond of union for all the Greeks, of whatever city or tribe, is a close and curious parallel to the evolution of Speculative out of Operative Masonry.

Another occupation that has always had something of the magical and uncanny about it is the craft of the metal worker. In the folk lore of Europe the blacksmith is always a character who is liable to do wonderful things, or who bargains with supernal or infernal powers on terms of equality. Wayland Smith is a well known hero of legend, and even Asa Thor was a smith and forged his own wonderful hammer. In the world over metals - and especially iron - have magical properties in themselves, they are "big medicine," and naturally the man who knows how to work them becomes invested with occult powers. The smiths of the Abyssinians, a caste apart, are also magicians. The gypsies of southeast Europe are fortune tellers and metal workers. The famous swords of Damascus were said to have been wrought with accompanying incantations and to have been tempered in human blood, while the swordsmiths of old Japan fasted and performed ceremonial rites of purification as a necessary preparation before beginning to forge a new masterpiece. And here incidently it may be noted that always in magical ceremonies the participants must divest themselves of everything of a metallic kind. And the root idea of this is probably that metal is a new fangled and disturbing element, and upsets the spirits and powers of the old primeval magic - the magic of bone and chipped flint. The special significance this may possibly have will be seen later.

THE BUILDERS USED MAGIC

So far we have found traces of primitive initiation rites becoming specialized and modified into what may be called "occupational" forms - agricultural, pastoral and shamanistic, and one still more specialized craft. But men as well as seeking food and making tools have always in some degree made shelters for themselves, that is, have been builders. And here we find ourselves deep in magic again. The spirits of the forest must be propitiated before a clearing can be made. The foundations must be marked out according to prescribed ritual - for luck. The earth must receive her due to ward off all the evil she might bring for the offense of violating the ground. Wherever we go, at whatsoever level of culture it may be, we find necessary observances and sacrifices to be made before it is safe to build, before the building is safe to use, before it is sure to stand. In Dahomey the pillars of the king's palace were dropped on living slaves in the holes dug to receive them. In the Pacific, prisoners were made to hold the corner posts of the chief's house and so buried alive. And as soon as people rise to a state of society complex enough to have specialized occupations, what is more natural than that those who follow the craft of building should become the custodians of the rites necessary for the safety of the structures they erect. The magic is as necessary as the technical skill. Of course this may remain in the gilds of magicians, as it apparently did among the Etruscans and the Romans, and as it still does among the Chinese. Yet in medieval legend it is always the Masons who build the child into the wall that their work may stand and the craft be honored thereby. And possibly even today in southeastern Europe the passer-by may have his shadow measured by stealth that the rod may be built into the wall of the new house - by which he will be sure to die within the year. Or the mortar in which the first bricks are laid may be mingled with the blood of a young cockerel. That such things were done is certain. That the builders were ignorant of them is incredible.

It may be as well at this point to re-capitulate the conclusions thus far reached. No attempt, it will have been noted, has been made to give the detailed facts on which the argument has been based. But this is certainly not because the various steps have all been hypothetical in character, but rather that the evidence has been collected in such masses that it is difficult to know how to select from it, and most of it is reasonably accessible, though of course it is not to be found all in one place, nor collected with a Masonic reference. We may then, without much risk, assume the following propositions. First: that what we call the magical was indiscriminately mixed with the practical in the activities of primitive men, though to his thinking all was equally practical. Second: that this magic, or at least its forms, has survived in various degrees and combinations in all higher cultures even to our own. Third: that this primitive collective magic especially tends to survive in institutions and select societies of the "Mystery" type. Fourth: that with the increasing complexity of the social structure, and the division and sub-divisions of functions and occupations, such institutions show in some cases a tendency to become occupational. Fifth: that of these occupational institutions and societies that of magicians or medicine men is practically universal. From this by further differentiation emerge in all the higher cultures, two professions - that of priest and physician. Other early and fundamental occupations are the agricultural and pastoral. And then, probably later than these, as specialized crafts, the trades of the metal worker and the builder.

BUILDING WAS ASSOCIATED WITH MANY TRADES

Now the term "builder" has been used intentionally because it is indeterminate. The type of building at any given time or place depends on two independently variable factors, both obvious - the material most available, and the level of general culture of the builders. But practically the material has always been wood, earth or stone.

The skin tents of nomads and the snow houses of the Esquimaux need hardly be considered since they are exceptional. But whatever the material used, or chiefly used, the fundamentals of building, both practical and magical, would be very much the same. Whatever may be the variations in form to be found the underlying principles are constant. From these primitive beginnings, wherever a people have risen above the barbaric level the more specialized crafts of carpenter, bricklayer or mason have appeared. All three, but especially the first and the last, use some form of striking implement - some form of axe or hammer - both evolved from the original hafted celt of the cave man. Both the axe and the hammer are the world over regarded as being in -themselves sanctities, full of mana or magic power.

Now as soon as more ambitious structures than mere temporary structures are attempted other tools are required - some form of measuring rod, or gauge, and some instrument to test angles. It is not at all necessary to suppose that these last were not independently invented and re-invented, many times, but the striking tools go back to the most primitive weapon of the earliest men of all, the rude hammer stone held in the hand.

So much then for the approach of this side. Let us now attack the problem in reverse. Our last step would indicate that it would be not only among masons that we should look for such survivals, but that they might also be expected among other crafts specifically connected with building. That this may actually have been the ase in medieval times two facts tend to show. In Scotland, the "wrights," who included carpenters, bricklayers and plasterers and so on had an institution and a form of reception called the "brithering" that on the outside sounds very like a description of what seventeenth century Operative Masonry may have been. The other is that in France the Compagnonnage seems in very early times to have included other trades connected with building, besides masons, and what may perhaps be the oldest branch seems at first to have been confined to carpenters.

Now this helps to remove a difficulty which if not always clearly discerned has always been in the way of tracing back the Masonic Fraternity to remote antiquity. Why was it that the men concerned in one particular trade, and a highly specialized one too, should have become the custodians of ancient mystic lore? But when we realize that the institution may not have been originally confined to

Masons only but was inherited, as it were, by them as being a sub-division of the whole craft of building the problem takes a new aspect; and we can see that while the medieval Freemason might even have developed and invented his undoubtedly new technique from the very beginning, that is, he need not have received his art directly from the stone masons of the preceding cultures of Rome and Greece (though a strong case can be made out for the hypothesis that he did) yet in any case he must have had a building tradition of some sort, behind him, in some style and material. The basis for the transmission of secret rites thus becomes pyramidal instead of columnar, a network instead of a single line.

That the rites of Freemasonry are archaic survivals seems to the present writer almost unquestionable. There are no real parallels to it among the usages of the trades gilds, and gilds merchant. The Compagnonnage offers only an apparent exception, for the admission of crafts unconnected with building is certainly of late date. The gilds, fraternities and like organizations of the Middle Ages were associations of convenience, for mutual profit and safety, exactly as are trades unions and manufacturers' associations today. With changing conditions they very generally disappeared. Freemasonry however still survives. Why? Surely only because it was more than a trades union - because of its ancient and magical initiation.

Here however two objections may be raised. It has been held by authorities of weight that the Third Degree and all it implies was invented and added to the "body of Masonry" by the scholarly brethren who were concerned in the re-organization of the Craft in 1717, or, in a variant of what is essentially the same hypothesis, by supporters of the Stuart cause in the seventeenth century. I have at some length given my reasons elsewhere for believing that Freemasonry as we know it is in its essentials of remote antiquity, though the present arrangement is certainly modern, as well as the greater part of the moral and symbolic explanations. One argument only need be touched on here. The legend of the Third Degree in its earliest known forms (as it is told today its archaic character is effectively masked) is not a thing that would be, or even could be, deliberately invented by civilized men - even with the aid "of sundry hints from the Targums," or the Kabbala, or anything else.

IS THERE MAGIC IN FREEMASONRY?

The second of the two objections that might be made is that there is nothing apparent of a magical character in Symbolic Masonry, and only the very slightest allusion to foundations in its ceremonies. But we could hardly expect anything else; anything that was very apparent could with difficulty have survived the successive expurgations and improvements to which our rites have been subjected in the last two hundred years. Yet even so the traces are more than a few. The non-use of metals occurs at once. This, according to the familiar explanation, is commemorative of the account of the building of the Temple without the sound of axe or hammer or any metal implement. This explanation is of course comparatively recent, but curiously this Biblical account is itself an instance of the same magical tabu. "To lift up a tool of iron" against a stone was to pollute it for religious use according to ancient Hebrew ideas. The force of the prohibition had broken down by Solomon's time, and yet, though the stones were wrought in the quarries, the form of the old tabu was in some sense preserved.

There is again the intense horror of old Masons generally (though not now universally it must be admitted) of any movement in the lodge "widdershins about," as the Scotch put it, that is, against the course of the sun. Another thing that might be mentioned is the very curious resemblance that the old "diagram" of the lodge (now rather inadequately represented by our charts and floor carpets) to the templum of the Roman augurs, and to the magic circles of medieval necromancers and others. But it is obvious that this is not an easy subject to discuss in public, and in any case would take too much space to go into it at all fully. The real argument is the resemblance in general of our ceremonies to primitive and magical rites.

Those to whom this is all entirely new may be inclined to doubt, and to ask why there should be such survivals. The full answer would be a treatise on social psychology, but as a short method of reply one might ask in return, Why is offering the hand a universally understood token of friendship and good will among us, or why is raising the hat an act showing respect? The circumstances under which these actions had an obvious meaning have long since passed away, yet they remain in full force as conventions. And our life is full of such conventions which are survivals of things that were once natural and obvious.

For any who, while admitting the existence of such survivals in custom, may yet doubt whether an organization existed secretly transmitting a system of such survivals could exist a very curious and interesting parallel can be pointed out; material has quite recently been collected to show that the witchcraft of the Middle Ages and even that of the New England states, was no sporadic superstition but was definitely though loosely organized (in a manner, by the way, remarkably resembling that of Masonic lodges meeting by inherent right) and that this organization was at times and in certain places so powerful that the authorities of Church and State had very good and practical reason to fear it. It appears in effect to have been the survival in full force of a primitive prechristian religion, whose deities were by the Church (very naturally) equated with the powers of darkness, and which in consequence more and more made a point that its adherents should in every way renounce Christianity utterly. And here it may be pointed out that the objection that the Church had to the Compagnonnage (in France) was that it concealed heresy, witchcraft and blasphemy - that is, enmity and antagonism to Christianity in itself. That Freemasons have been very freely accused, in some countries, of worshipping Satan is of course a ridiculous slander - and yet it is not absolutely invented out of whole cloth, for it was long popularly supposed, after the emergence of the Institution into publicity early in the eighteenth century, that Freemasons "raised the devil" in their lodges. This opinion of the populace may well have been passed along from times long anterior to the historical period of the Order, though it may quite likely have been kept alive by deliberate mystification on the part of convivial and jocular brethren.

The gilds died when their raison d'etre ceased, when the conditions in society that had called them forth had passed away. Freemasonry on the other hand was not extinguished even by laws aimed, in part at least, specifically at its suppression as an organization. This suggests that the gild (of Masons) and the lodge were entirely separate and distinct entities, even where the membership was identical. And this further might prove a clue to the solution of some other puzzles. But what was it that continued to hold Masons together working and honorary, Operative and Speculative, in spite of legislation and social change? Perhaps the power of the magic of primitive man always lay in the social and collective emotion in which all the participants in the rites felt a mysterious bond of union with each other and with something, undefined and vague, greater than anyone of them. Perhaps after all we have done little more than re-name and re-classify these things. We refer it all to psychology instead of magic, while the original reality still remains as potent as ever.

NOTES

1. The account of the "brithering" of the "wrights" is to be found in Lyon's History of the Old Lodge of Edinburgh. But the reference is given also in Gould's History.

2. The best known authority on the Compagnonnage is Perdiguier, whose works, however, are very rare. The substance of his account is to be found in Gould's History. Lionel Vibert's monograph (A.I.C.) on the subject should also be consulted.

3. Tyler-Keystone for March and April, 1915, under heading "The Sublime Degree".

4. Most works on folk lore have references to this subject. The authorities quoted in the note to the article on the "Great Journey" in THE BUILDER, present volume, page 274, are all useful. The best collection of material on circumambulations is Simpson's "Buddhist Prayer Wheel".

5. The Witch Cult in Western Europe (author's name forgotten!), published 1922.

On the Mysteries in general there has of late years been much written, but most of it rather scattered. Besides the Golden Bough, see Lang's Myth Ritual and Religion and Simpson's Jonah Legend. Miss Harrison's Themis and Cook's Zeus may be consulted.

Language of the Heart
Carl H. Claudy

FREEMASONRY TEACHES BY SYMBOLS!

Why? Why does she veil in allegory and conceal in an object or picture a meaning quite different from its name?

Why should Freemasonry express Immortality with Acacia, Brotherly Love with a Trowel, the World by a Lodge and Right Living by a Mason's

That Freemasonry conceals in symbols in order to arouse curiosity to know their meaning is often considered the only explanation. But there are many more lofty ideas of why this great system of truth, philosophy and ethics is hidden in symbols.

It is hardly a matter of argument that man has a triple nature; he has a body and senses which bring him into contact with and translate the meanings of the physical world of earth, air, fire and water which is about him. He has a brain and a mind by which he reasons and understands about the matters physical with which he is surrounded. And he has a Something Beyond; call it Soul, Heart, Spirit or imagination, as you will; it is something which is allied to, rather than a part of reason, and connected with the physical side of life only through its sensory contacts.

This soul, or spirit, comprehends a language which the brain does not understand. The keenest minds have striven without success to make this mystic language plain to reason. When you hear music which brings tears to your eyes and grief or joy to your heart, you respond to a language your brain does not understand and cannot explain. It is not with your brain that you love your mother, your child or your wife; it is with the Something Beyond; and the language with which that love is spoken is not the language of the tongue.

A symbol is a word in that language. Translate that symbol into words which appeal only to the mind, and the spirit of the meaning is lost. Words appeal to the mind; meanings not expressed in words appeal to the spirit.

All that there is in Freemasonry, which can be set down in words on a page, leaves out completely the Spirit of the Order, If we depend upon words or ideas alone, the Fraternity would not make a universal appeal to all men, since no man has it given to him to appeal to minds of all other men. But Freemasonry expresses truths which are universal; it expresses them in a universal language, universally understood by all men without words. That language is the language of the symbol, and the symbol is universally understood because it is the means of communication between spirit, souls and hearts.

When we say of Masonry that it is universal we mean the word literally; it is of the universe, not merely of the world. If it were possible for an inhabitant of Mars to make and use a telescope which would enable him to plainly see a square mile of the surface of the earth, and if we knew it and desired to, we could draw upon that square mile a symbol to communicate with that inhabitant of Mars, we would choose, undoubtedly, one with as many meanings as possible; one which had a material, mental and spiritual meaning. Such a symbol might be the triangle, the square or the circle. Our supposed Martian might respond with a complimentary symbol; if we showed him a triangle he might reply with the 47th Problem. If we showed him a circle he might send down 3.141659 - the number by which a diameter is multiplied to become the circumference. We could find a language in symbols with which to begin a communication, even with all the universe!

Naturally then, Freemasonry employs symbols for heart to speak to heart. Imagination is the heart's collection of senses. So we must appeal to the imagination when speaking a truth which is neither mental nor physical, and the symbol is the means by which one imaginations speaks to another. Nothing else will do; no words can be as effective (unless they are themselves symbols); no teachings expressed in language can be as easily learned by the heart as those which come via the symbol through the imagination.

Take from Masonry its symbols and you have just the husk; the kernel is gone. He who hears but the words of Freemasonry misses their meaning entirely. Most symbols have many interpretations. These do not contradict but amplify each other. Thus, the square is a symbol of perfection, rectitude of conduct, honor, honesty and good work. There are all different and yet allied. The square is not a symbol of wrong, evil, meanness or disease! Ten different men may read ten different meanings into a square, and yet each meaning fits with and belongs to the other meanings.

Ten men have ten different kinds of hearts. Not all have the same power of imagination. They do not all have the same ability to comprehend. So each gets from a symbol what he can. He uses his imagination. He translates to his soul as much of the truth as he is able to make a part of him. This the ten cannot do with truths expressed in words. "Twice two is equal to four" is a truth which must be accepted all at once, as a complete exposition, or not at all. He who can not understand the "twice" or the "equal" or the "four" has no conception of what is being said. But ten men can read ten progressive, different, correct and beautiful meanings into a trowel, and each can be right as far as he goes. The man who sees it merely as an instrument which helps to bind has a part of its meaning. He who finds it a link with operative Masons has another part. The man who sees it as a symbol of man's relationship to Deity, because with it he (spiritually) does the Master's Work, has another meaning. All these meanings are right; when all men know all the meanings the need for Freemasonry will have passed away.

We use symbols because only by them can we speak the language of the spirit, each to each, and because they form an elastic language, which each man reads for himself according to his ability. Symbols form the only language which is thus elastic, and the only one by which spirit can be touched. To suggest that Freemasonry use any other would be as revolutionary as to remove her Altars, meet in a Public Square or elect by majority vote. Freemasonry without symbols would not be Freemasonry; it would be but a dogmatic and not very erudite philosophy, of which the world is full of as it is, and none of which ever satisfies the heart.

Toleration and Freethinking

H.L. Haywood

A certain amount of ambiguity attaches to these two terms because they are so often used as if one meant the same thing as the other, a notion that is very erroneous, as it is the purpose of my brief study to show. This subject is, not merely an academic one, as a few experiences of the recent war period have reminded us. At the present moment there are hundreds of persons in our penitentiaries who exercised what was, as they supposed, the constitutional right to think and express themselves according to their own convictions. And there are some groups, such as the Pacifists, who, during the war, plead hard for tolerance, which to them was the right to exist. These, and many kindred matters, have aroused much interest among Masons, for there is no doctrine in the teachings of the Craft that has been more prominently advocated than the doctrine of toleration. "Thou shalt not persecute a man for differing from thee in opinion," has been a foremost Masonic commandment for these two hundred years. When Albert Pike rebuilt the ritual of the Scottish Rite he gave the doctrine such prominence that to some members of that body it is chief among their teachings. Accordingly there is such a coincidence between the interest that the war period has aroused in the subject and the interest that all Masons have ever felt in it, that an attempt, such as the present, to examine even briefly and informally, the meaning of these ideas, is not altogether an office of vain endeavor.

Toleration is at best a negative thing. It means that if you differ from me I shall not molest you, though I may at the same time have no respect for your thoughts and little desire to permit you to go on thinking. Oftentimes I will not molest you, not because I believe you to have a right to think, but because I may fear my inability to worst you, or may believe a conflict not worth its cost. Toleration can go along with the denial of the right of free thought where an organization or where society feels itself too powerful to be made subject to danger by what anybody thinks. In Hyde Park London, men are permitted to utter their wildest ideas, often of a most anarchistic character, while policemen stand by to preserve order for them, and the government takes no notice, because it is too secure to be endangered by the cries of a few demagogues.

It is not uncommon to find men who believe that during the medieval period the church denied to each and all the right to do their own thinking about religion. This is an error, for there was a vast amount of differing opinions in that time, but the church did not often persecute individuals because it was too confident of its own powers to worry about them. There was then a great deal of toleration practiced, but it did not therefore justify the doctrine of freethinking, for that is an entirely different doctrine. Those who are familiar with the history of Scholasticism, and more particularly with certain leaders thereof, such as Aquinas, Duns Scotus, Abelard, etc., know how wide a latitude such thinkers enjoyed, and how free they were in the expression of many opinions at variance with the official creed of the church. But it was toleration these men enjoyed, not the true rights of freethinking. In the period of the Renaissance even the popes began to speculate in a very unorthodox manner, and as for cardinals, bishops, and theologians, they set loose a veritable anarchy of new speculation. All this was tolerated, but it was not freethinking, for at that very time the church was claiming its own infallibility, and the principles of Jesuitism were fast becoming orthodox. In all these cases the church was too confident of its own powers to much fear the innovators, and it accordingly left them to talk and think at will, as a mother will not interfere with the children playing about her knee, so long as they do not go too far.

From the point of view of those who receive it, toleration is merely the right to exist, which is not much of a right. The Waldenses, for example, were tolerated for a long time. This does not mean that the authorities admitted for one moment that the Waldenses enjoyed the same right of determining religious rites and theories as that enjoyed by the church; it only means that until the Waldenses grew to such dimensions as threatened to disturb the authority and integrity of the church they were permitted to exist.

Toleration, as I said above, is negative in its very nature; it only means that I shall not persecute you for disagreeing with me. It is a condescension made by a superior power and it is therefore often felt to be a disgrace, even though the inferior power gladly avails itself of such privileges as it confers. When we talk about toleration in Masonry, it is not such a thing that we have in mind. That kind of thing is not something to be proud of; it is not a thing for which men gladly fight; it is not in itself a fruitful principle out of which culture, manhood, and power can grow.

In toleration the right of free thought is merely permitted.
In freethinking the right of free thought is encouraged.

This is the difference between the two, and it is because of this difference that I said a while ago that flee thought is a positive thing. I use my own mind in searching for truth: I encourage you to use your mind in the same way: the two of us encourage others to think for themselves. In such a situation this there is no dominant power, no controlling institution, no commanding creed, which is so sure of its own ability to control the field that it grants privileges to minority that it does not fear. Free thought and toleration are not two sides of the same idea, they are two essentially different ideas, and even, to some extent, opposed to each other.

It is necessary here to guard our minds against confusing the doctrine of free thought with that group of men who during the middle of the last century, over threw the doctrines of Christianity and set up a set of their own doctrines instead, and who carried in a well defined propaganda with courses of lectures, a publishing house, headquarters, etc. In their case "Free-thinker" was a party name, and carried with it the obligations of a kind of creed. Freethinking here use carries no reference to that group of men: it does not mean that if we become freethinkers we must straight- way begin to buy the publications of the Rationalist Press Association. One may enjoy the prerogatives of free thought without agreeing at all with Leslie Stephen, J. R. Robertson, Thomas Huxley, Ernest Haeckel et al (I speak not disparagingly of these men, however: I have a great regard for them all.)

In the doctrine of freethinking (as here interpreted, at any rate) there are two well-defined ideas. One of these is that there is not anywhere any institution or book, or creed, or set of men who have the absolute truth, and who may grant or withhold to others rights to differ. No such custodian of truth exists anywhere in any church, or book, or creed, or group. There can be no private property or vested interest in the truth To search for the truth, to define the truth, to promulgate the truth, is a task for us all; and every one of us, be he the humblest of the lot, has the same inherent right in the premises as the greatest of all.

The point here made may be well illustrated by two episodes out of the history of science. When the Italian anatomist, Vesalius, undertook his pioneer work in dissecting the human body, the ecclesiastical authorities opposed him with the authority of Aristotle and of Galen.

Vesalius was told that these two wise masters had settled all matters of anatomy and that he was a trespasser on a field belonging to others: if he would devote himself to the service of these masters, and would remain content, as was true of other so-called anatomists of the period, to be an expositor of the theories of Aristotle and Galen, he would be permitted to work on unmolested. The authorities wished to grant him tolerance; what he claimed was the right of free investigation. To get that right he was obliged to leave Italy.

Another episode to point the same moral is found in the experience of Copernicus and of Galileo. When these two astronomers appeared upon the scene it was everywhere taken for granted that Aristotle (Aristotle was an intellectual god during the Middle Ages) and Ptolemy had said the last word in astronomy; their teachings had been accepted into the authoritative creed of the church. Copernicus was cried down as a vain fool; Galileo was forced into prison and made to recant. Both men, under certain conditions, were granted a certain tolerance: neither was given the right of free thought. The rights of free thought were impossible so long as it was supposed that astronomical truth reposed in the keeping of Ptolemy and Aristotle.

The other of the two ideas implied in the doctrine of freethinking is that truth itself can never be found except as a trophy won by the action of all men's minds. It is the very nature of truth that it cannot be granted to us by any specific revelation; or that it can be discovered and possessed by any one man or group of men; be that man prophet, scientist, or priest; be that group academy, university, church, or lodge. Truth is found after many searchings; it is arrived at through many discoveries; it must be approached from every corner of the compass: all must cooperate in the search for it or it cannot be found. When men are denied the right to think for themselves the doors that lead to the truth automatically close themselves. And insofar as we desire to find the truth should we not alone permit, but encourage, and that in all ways, every man to think his best, to keep his own eyes open, to speak what he thinks, and to act as wisdom and experience dictate? For any man, or set of men, to climb to a platform above all the rest of us, and from that eminence to look down upon us, to direct our goings, and to dictate our thinking, is not only an injustice, it is a folly: for such a procedure always sets back civilization.

If all this be true, why did a democratic government like our own throw Eugene Debs into prison, and make war on Victor Berger? In their thinking about the war, we may suppose, those men disagreed with the United States Congress: should they not have been entitled to differ? Have we not free thought in America? Why was it that so many Masons opposed the activities of the Socialist Party and believed that Debs received that which he deserved?

The answer to this lies in the fact that there is a necessary distinction between speech that serves as an expression of ideas, and speech that is a form of action. Debs, Berger, and their fellows might have talked and thought until now without interference; inherent justice as well as the Constitution granted them that right: they might also have tried to persuade others to think as they were thinking. But that is not what they did. What they did was, by means of speeches, to obstruct the draft. Their speeches were made, not as expressions of opinion, but as forms of action, and such actions necessarily were bound by the laws governing the actions of us all. If I stand on a street corner to persuade a crowd of bystanders that your opinions are erroneous and that my opinions are better, I am enjoying the privilege of free speech; my talking comes under that head, and is to be dealt with accordingly. But if I stand on that same street corner to incite that crowd to go down with me to burn your house over your head, that speech is not properly speech but action, for it has all the consequences of action. It is for lack of making this obvious and necessary distinction that so many have grown confused about the rights of free speech, free thought, and free action.

Regenberg Stonemason's Regulations
A New Translation from the German
F. W. Kracher

(The historic document herewith presented is a new translation of the oldest Regulations of the German Stonemasons — or
Steinmetzen — dating from 1459. The original German, as quaint as
the English of Chaucer, may be found in *Die Romanische* and *Gothische
Architektur*, by Max Hasak, published at Stuttgart 1902. Other documents of the kind fall chiefly in the time of the German Renaissance,
and present nothing but unimportant extensions or modifications of
the first Regensburg Regulation. They are mainly as follows: — the
Strassburg Regulation of 1459, the *Torgau* of 1462, the *Basle* of 1497, the
so-called *Brothers' Book* of 1563, and the *Querfurt Regulation* of 1574.
Further, there were different records of the original Regulation, such
as those of Vienna, of Admont and the Tyrol Regulation of 1480.

This interesting document brings up the question, so hotly
debated in Masonic literature, as to the relation of the German
Steinmetzen to the Guilds on the one hand, and to the Freemasons on
the other. English writers, like Speth, go so far as to deny to the Stone-
masons any esoteric lore, while German scholars, like Krause, Findel
and Steinbrenner, insist that they were Freemasons. Of course this
question cannot be discussed in an introductory note, but we shall
have something to say about it in due time. Meanwhile, with this
debatable question in mind, the Brethren will find these old Regulations a very profitable study if they will read them in the light of
what Brother Gould has to say in his *"Concise History of Masonry,"* (pp
42-62) and on the other side the discussions of Findel and Steinbrenner
in their histories of the Craft.)

In the name of the Father, the Son, the Holy Spirit, and the
mother Mary and also her saintly servants, crowned in honor of the
holy quartet, be it stated that genuine friendship, harmony and obedience is the foundation of all virtues. For the common good and for
the information of all princes, nobles, lords, cities, founders, and
monasteries who are now erecting churches or other large buildings
of stone or may erect such buildings in the future, this is written, so

that each one may know his rights and privileges. It is also written for the benefit of all master masons and journeymen throughout the German lands, who are especially desirous to keep the Craft clean from all discord, jealousy, care, expense, and harm. Some of the regulations which the fathers had drawn up with the best intentions are being misused by both, masters and workers, and they no longer endeavor to adhere to the rules. To change this condition, delegations of master masons and workers met at Spyr, Strassburg, and Regensburg with power to act for the Craft. The old existing rules were renewed and somewhat purified, thereby bringing all peacefully together. After the regulations had been written down we solemnly promised not only to keep them ourselves but to enforce them in the future among the followers of the stonemason craft. The rules are as follows:

1. Whoever finds any of the rules in this regulation too severe or too lenient may, in accordance with the conditions of the time or the country, add to or subtract from them. Any change must neither disturb the arrangement nor the spirit of the original rules and must then be faithfully observed by all.

2. Any stonemason who has the desire to join our order, for which this book is written, must promise (swear) to keep all the separate rules of our regulation. Master masons shall be those who can erect a stone structure according to a plan. They do not have to do actual work with their own hands unless they so desire. Whether they are masters or journeymen, they ought to conduct themselves honorably, harm no one in his rights, and in case of necessity are to be punished in accordance with the rules laid down.

3. Buildings which are erected at present and where the workmen are paid by the day are, Strassburg, Cologne, Vienna, and Passan, also in the workshops belonging to the same. Day wages shall continue in connection with these buildings and in no way shall the contract system be used, so that no interruption in the work arises due to the change from the day labor system to the contract system.

4. In case of death of any stonemason employed on a regular building, it is permissible that any workman or master, capable of doing the work, apply for the vacancy. In this manner the supervisors of the work shall find a proper successor. The same rule applies also to a journeyman who understands stone masonry.

5. If a master should accept a second job, or any master who is not occupied accept a new job, it is their duty to start work by the day immediately so that no discredit may come to the craft. Should trustworthy parties lodge complaint against a master as to the work or the employment of a certain kind of labor, then he shall be tried and punished according to the rules. The complainant may not carry his case that far but simply demand that the master begin the work either by the day or contract. The master must then act according to the suggestion.

6. If a master in charge of some work dies and another master steps in his place and finds prepared stones either placed in position in the wall or not, he is not allowed to remove placed stones nor to discard loose ones. This is necessary so that employers may not be subjected to unnecessary expense, and that the master who did the work may not be criticized. Should the employer wish to remove stones it may be permitted as long as no danger to the structure arises therefrom.

7. A master shall not hire out his masons for any other work except such which is directly connected with the hewing of stones. He may use them for breaking stone, lime, or sand by the day or by the job without danger of reproach.

8. In case masons are needed either to hew stones or to set them, the master may shift them. Those so shifted are not subject to the rules set forth as long as they do it on their own accord and willingly.

9. Two masters shall not jointly supervise a job or a building unless it be a small building which can be finished within a year. Such a job may be undertaken with a partner.

10. If a master accepts a contract according to the submitted specifications he must not change anything. The work must be done according to the specifications which he submitted to the employers, cities, or to the country. This will prevent the weakening of any part of the work.

11. If there be any master or journeyman who attempts to force a master, who is conducting a job under these regulations, out of his position, he shall be tried. The same is to be done if one openly or secretly intrigues against any master without his knowledge. No master mason or journeyman shall associate with him, and no craftsman belonging to the order shall work for him as long as he is busy

with the job wrongfully obtained. This is to continue until the one forced out of the job shall be reinstated and explanations given him by the committee of master masons appointed for this purpose by the order.

12. If any one should attempt to break stone without having previously served as a regular workman and acquired some shop training, his stones must not be accepted by anyone. In case some one should do so, then no journeyman must stand by him or go with him, so that employers are not given unnecessary expense thru such an unwise master.

13. No workman or master, neither parlierer (instructor) nor journeyman shall instruct anyone, not a stonemason, from any manual unless the instructor be a member of the craft.

14. No workman or master shall take any money from a journeyman for teaching him something concerning stone-masonry. No parlierer (instructor) or journeyman shall instruct for money. If one wishes to show or teach something to others he may do so step by step for fellow-workman's sake.

15. Any master having charge of a building may have three helpers, either master masons or journeymen. If he has more than one building he shall not have more than two helpers on the second building. Not more than five helpers shall be employed on both buildings

16. No master or workman shall be taken into the order who does not receive the holy sacrament at least once a year, or who does not observe the Christian rules of conduct, or who gambles. In case such an unfit person did by chance get into the order, no master mason should have any association with him whatsoever. No workman should work for him unless he turns from his old ways and has been punished by those who are in the order.

17. No workman or master mason should be adulterous. Should one insist upon such a course, no journeyman or stonemason should work for him or associate with him.

18. If a fellow craft accepts work with a master who has not yet been raised to the rank of overseer in the order, he shall not be subject to a punishment. He may very well do so because each craftsman should seek advancement. The workman should keep the rules of the order although he is not working in a regulation shop or for a brother of the order. Should one take a wife unto himself and not

work in a regulation shop but settle down in a city where he had to work at a craft, he will have to pay four pennies poll- tax but be free of any other tax, as long as he does not work in a regular shop.

19. In case a complaint is made by one master against another master that he acted against the rules of the order; or by a master against a craftsman, or by a craftsman against another, it shall be brought to a master who has been appointed to handle such cases. Both sides shall be heard, and then a day set when the case will be considered. During the time up to the trial no controversy whatsoever shall take place between master and worker until the case has been settled. The decision shall be given by masters, and this decision must be carried out. The case is to be tried where it arose by the master in whose jurisdiction it happened.

20. A "parlierer" shall respect his master and obey him willingly in everything pertaining to the craft. The same shall be done by the fellowcraft.

21. If a journeyman decides to travel on, he should depart from his master and the shop without any complaint against him, and leaving no debts, whatsoever, behind.

22. Any journeyman, in whatever kind of a shop he shall be employed, ought to be obedient to the "parlierer" and his master in everything pertaining to the craft.

23. And he shall not scold about the master's work secretly nor publicly, unless the master were to act contrary to the rules of the order.

24. Every workman who has received the power to enforce the rules of the order in all disputes touching upon stonemasons and masonry, has also the power to bring to trial and to decide upon punishment. All masters, parlierers, and craftsmen shall be obedient to him.

25. Even though a craftsman has journeyed and worked as a stonemason and made advancement in the order, he should not be accepted by a master if this experience be less than two years, and if he only wanted to do a little work.

26. Masters and workers belonging to this order shall obey all the rules of this regulation. Should one or the other break any one of the rules he is not to be punished if he repents and promises to keep the rule in the future.

27. A master having charge of a book of the order shall take care of it according to his vow to the order. He must not copy it nor have it copied by someone else, he must not give it or lend it to any person, so that the book may always remain with the craft as the workers decided. But, if a member of the order should need to know a paragraph or two, these may be given to him by the master in writing. The master shall arrange to have the rules read aloud to all workers in the shops once every year.

28. If the question arise whether any member under complaint shall be expelled, the master of the district shall not act independently. Two other masters who are in possession of the written rules, and who are empowered by their brethren, shall be summoned so that the council is made up of three. To this council shall be added the workers of the shop in which the trouble arose. The decision of the three masters, supported by the majority of the workers shall then be accepted by all the craftsmen.

29. In case two or more masters of the order should quarrel over affairs not directly connected with stone-masonry, this quarrel shall not be brought before any other court but that of the order, which shall decide in accordance with their understanding. The decision must, however, be submitted to the cities in which the quarrel took place, for approval.

30. That the ritual of the order may be properly observed with divine worship and other necessary ceremonies, each master shall donate to the order one "gulden" at his initiation. Hereafter he is to pay four "blappart" (small silver coin) annually into the treasury of the order. Each craftsman also pays four "blapparts"; the same every apprentice after finishing his term.

31. Each master and workman belonging to the order and employed in a shop, shall be in possession of a savings-box. Into this box shall be dropped one penny each week. The money is to be collected by the master and handed to the order once a year. With it shall be paid the church services and other expenses of the order.

32. All masters who have such boxes but in whose shops there is kept no book-(of account) of the order, shall hand it to the master who has the books once a year, and a church-service is to follow. If a master or craftsman dies in a shop where no book is kept, this must be reported to the next master who has a book of the order. After being informed of such a death, he shall have a mass read for the

benefit of the departed soul, and the master and craftsmen who had worked with the deceased are to pay for it.

33. Any expense caused to a master or craftsman by the order shall be refunded out of the order's treasury; may it be little or much. If any one were to be brought before court in affairs pertaining to the order, or if one were thereby thrown into need, all masters and craftsmen should aid him in accordance with their vow to the order.

34. In case a master or craftsman becomes ill, or has to discontinue the work and is, thereby, confronted by need, he shall receive assistance from those masters having charge of the order's treasury. The one receiving help must, however, promise to repay all money received after his recovery. In case of death, so much of the clothing and other articles left behind, shall be sold, as is necessary to cover the debt.

This is the regulation book of the watchers (foremen) and craftsmen.

35. No master shall employ a craftsman who has induced a woman to adultery, or who leads an immoral life with women; who does not go to confession at least once a year as the church prescribes, or who has the evil reputation of gambling his clothes away.

36. If any workman ask unnecessarily for a leave of absence, he shall forfeit his privilege for another leave for one whole year. This applies to workmen in the shops and also such employed on the buildings.

37. If any master employs a traveling craftsman and wishes to discharge him, he may do so on a Saturday or the evening of payday, so that the man may be able to travel on. The same shall be done by a craftsman who wishes to leave. This rule does not hold good if just cause was given by either side.

38. No craftsman shall approach any one else for work except it be the master of the job or the overseer, and never without his master's or the overseer's knowledge.

Regulation of the Servants (Common Laborers.)

39. A master shall not employ any laborer who has not been born in wedlock. He must, therefore, endeavor to inform himself accordingly by asking the man whether his father and mother were really and truly married.

40. No builder or master shall make any laborer, who is still serving as an apprentice, a "parlierer" (watchman.)

41. No builder or master shall make any laborer a "parlierer" although he may have served his term as an apprentice, but who has not at least traveled one year.

42. If one has served as assistant to a mason and comes to a master, in order to learn from him the craft, he shall not be accepted as an apprentice unless he is to serve as such an assistant for three years.

43. No builder or master shall employ anyone as laborer and raise him to a finished apprentice within less than five years.

44. Should it happen that an apprentice leaves his master during his term without just cause, that apprentice shall not be employed by any other master. No fellow craftsman shall support him or associate with him in any way unless he can show testimonial that he has served the regular time and met all the requirements of the master. No one shall buy himself free before the time, unless he entered into marriage with the consent of his master, or who has some other just cause which may force him or the master to do so.

45. Should a laborer think that he is not treated rightly by his master for whom he is working, he may bring complaint in the place where he is at work, so that he may receive instruction and the wrong may be righted in accordance with the rules of the order.

46. Each master who has a book (permission) from the district of Strassburg, shall pay each Christmas a half gulden into the treasury of Strassburg. And this shall be done so long until the debt is paid which stands against that treasury.

47. Any master who has a book and whose work has completed so that he cannot employ his helpers any longer, shall send the book and all the money which belongs to the order to the builder at Strassburg.

48. On St. Marc's day, in the year of our Lord one thousand four hundred and fifty nine, four weeks after Easter, the following was decided upon in the meeting at Regensburg: The builder Jost Dotzinger, of Worms, in charge of the cathedral of "Our Lady" at Strassburg, shall be the highest judge of our order. The same shall be true in the case of his successors at the same work. (A similar decision was given before at Spyr, at Strassburg, and on the ninth day of April, in the year fourteen hundred and sixty four again at Spyr.) Master Lorenz Spenning, of Vienna, shall be the highest authority at Vienna for the whole country.

The present masters at Strassburg, Vienna, and Cologne, these three, or their successors shall constitute the highest authority of the order. They cannot be displaced without good and just cause.

49. This is the district which belongs to Strassburg: All the country above the Mosel; the country of the Franks down to the Thuringian forest, and Babenburg to the monastery near Eystetten; from Eystetten to Ulm, from Ulm to Augsburg, to the Adelburg near land of the Welsh (Flance); Meisen, Thuringia, Saxony, Frankfurt, and Hesse, and also Swabia shall be obedient to him.

To the district of Master Lorenz Spenning, builder of the cathedral St. Stephan, at Vienna, belong: Lambach, Styria, Werckhusen, Hungaria (along the Danube.)

Master Steffen Hurder, builder of St. Vincent at Bern, shall control the cantons.

Master Conrad, of Cologne, builder of the cathedral at that place, and all his successors, shall have charge over the rest of the shops which are now in the order or may, in a future period, be admitted to the same

50. Any master, parlierer, and fellow-craftsman, acting contrary to a secret or recorded paragraph, shall be called before such a council and reprimanded, if the complaint is founded on good authority. Any punishment meted out must be obediently complied with, as the vow demands. If one disregards the call without a good reason, he shall be fined in absentia. If he refuses to pay he may be brought before a secular or ecclesiastical court which shall decide what ought to be done to him.

51. Whoever wants to join this order, must vow to keep all rules which are written in this book or may be added in the future. Should the emperor, king, prince or any other authority, rightly or wrongly, object to his belonging to the order, he may act in such a manner that no harm can come to him. Any business with the order can be arranged thru fellow-workmen who are members of the order.

52. If it is every Christian's duty to work at his soul's salvation, it is much more so a duty of every master and craftsman whom the almighty God has endowed with the ability, to erect churches and other buildings and, thereby, to earn their living. Thankfulness should fill their hearts, and prompted by their Christian nature they should endeavor to increase the divine services, and by doing so earn their soul's salvation. Therefore, in honor of God Almighty, his wor-

thy mother Mary, all the saints, and especially in honor of the holy four, and for the benefit of the souls of all persons who belong to this order or may join in the future, we, as stone-masons, have agreed upon these rules for ourselves and all our descendants: We will have celebrated one mass every year at the time dedicated to the holy four, namely in the munster at Strassburg, and there in the Chapel of Our Lady. This mass shall be one for our souls with all the ceremonies belonging to it.

53. This has been decided upon on the ninth day of April, in the year of our Lord one thousand four hundred and sixty four, in the representative meeting at Spyr, etc." (Then follows the names of the masters of the different delegations and their signatures and subscriptions.)

Hysteria in Freemasonry
WM. F. Kuhn

There is a certain mental condition, as set forth frequently in our Masonic literature, especially in that great forum, the Masonic press, that gives strong evidence of what may be termed Hysteria. It has not attained to that solidarity that we can characterize it as hysterical Freemasonry; it has such a spasmodic, fantastic and grotesque manifestation, that the term hysteria in Freemasonry is more suggestive, and at the same time relieves the fraternity of the onus of the disease and places it on the individual.

Freemasonry must not be held responsible for it, either by heredity or by environment; it is purely an exotic growth. Hysteria has been defined as, "Repressed Desire"; hence it is purely a mental state. We find hysteria in medicine, in religion, in law, in Pedagogics, in philosophy, in fact it abounds in all systems of thought. It should not, therefore, be thought strange that this mental quirk, this cerebration cut on the bias, should manifest itself in Freemasonry. The disease is not contagious in the accepted sense of the word, but it is transmitted by mimicry. If a circus comes to town and the boys succeed in attending it, the barns and woodsheds are filled for months, thereafter, by embryo rope walkers, contortionists and bare back riders. A transmission by imitation. It is equally true in Freemasonry; let some one expound something that looks, tastes, smells and sounds profound, imitators will spring up from all quarters. The more incomprehensible the seeming profundity, the greater the number of gymnasts in the Masonic barns and woodsheds. I have always believed that Freemasonry was a very practical thing; a something that manifests itself, chiefly, in a man's life; that it is a life and not a theory; practical living and doing, not dreaming and philosophizing. That it was a beautiful, everyday, practical system of morality veiled in allegory, and illustrated by symbols; not veiled to confuse or hide, but to make plain; not buried in symbols to obscure, but to fix indelibly some plain, possibly homely, truth. I have believed that the allegory and the symbol in Freemasonry stood in the same relation to the candidate that the parables of the "Great Teacher" stood in relation to the multitudes who heard Him. The allegory, the symbol and the parable are but different modes of expression to make clear the thought. But now comes the Masonic Philosopher and the Masonic Symbologist with eyes in fiery frenzy rolling, actuated and influenced by this "Repressed desire" and says: "It is all a mistake, Freemasonry is not such a simple thing, as everyday living and doing; no it is a sublime, profound system of metaphysics, that only the Ancient wise men understood and could explain; a philosophy so obscure that the average Mason, and, possible, a Past Grand Master, is a mere babe and suckling in the comprehension of it. I once met a man in a lunatic asylum, who came to me with crude geometrical figures of a sphere, a cube, an equilateral triangle, and a right angle triangle, drawn on the bottom of a paste board box. He explained to me that the three sides of the equilateral triangle represented the three great forces of Nature, namely, the upsideness, the downsideness and the downupsideness or the upsidedownness; as long as the upsideness and downsideness maintain their proper relation and were greater in power than the third side represented by the downupsideness or the upsidedownness, everything would be harmonious; but should these three great forces ever become projected, so as to form a right angle triangle, so that the square of the downsideupness or the upsidedownness becomes equal to the sum of the squares of the upsideness and downsideness, then chaos and evil would reign, and as the cube, representing the universe, consists of many right angle triangles, there would be an endless disturbance in the cosmogony of the world. I admired his vast learning and profundity, and I was mere suckling to his theme and theory. I advised him to write it out in full and that I would give him the names of several Masonic papers which would be more than delighted to publish it. This man had been judged insane, he was not a hysteric.

A Masonic hysteric is a man with a wild imagination plus a symbol. The beauty about a symbol, is its flexibility; you can see more things in it and through it than were ever dreamed of by mortal man, and no man can say to you, nay. It is said that a Masonic hysteric one day saw some rabbit tracks in the snow and he immediately began to demonstrate the fact that the rabbit had a working knowledge of the Omniscience, Omnipresence and Omnipotence of Deity, because the tracks were triangular in outline.

What I may have said may sound jestingly, but we need not go far to see the convulsions of these hysterics. I quote one from a leading Masonic Journal; listen to its profoundity: — "Therefore when we consider the profound truths, marvelous philosophy, and exact sciences upon which Freemasonry is founded, and which bear the ear marks of centuries of scientific research, such as the careful observer must admit is contained in the work, we must banish for all time the thought that the Craft was founded by any others than Masters of the Great School of Natural Science and Philosophy who permitted it to be known to the profane that the Guild or Craft was one of operative Masons, for the purpose only to hide the real truths and its true object from those hostile to the institution. This object was and has been for centuries to give to the human race TRUTH concerning the creation of the universe and the continuity of life after death, the immortality of the soul, and the relation which exists between this planet and the inhabitants of the whole universe. These truths are founded upon exact science, demonstrable by the Master in the possession of the knowledge, the whole being figured out on geometrical lines. Naturally this truth would come in conflict with orthodox and dogmatic religion."

His first claim is, that Freemasonry did not spring from the operative Mason and the history of such an ancestry was used merely as a blind behind which the Masters of the Great School of Natural Science and Philosophy hid themselves from hostile foes. No one will deny that the so called philosophy was engrafted into Masonry with the evolution of the Royal Arch. Many of the symbols and emblems in the Lodge Ritual were added during the period of Ritualistic development by Clare, Dunkerly, Hutchinson and Preston, but to claim that the Great Masters stole the livery of the Operative Craft as a mask through fear of hostility is absurd and unworthy of consideration, and it is to be regretted that the simple philosophy of right living should be perverted into an occult science and paraded as Masonic.

But the sum and substance of this "Repressed desire" is, that Freemasonry is a science plus a philosophy, which, when applied along "Geometrical lines," we may know the truth that will reveal to us immortality, the continuity of life after death, and the relation that exists between us and the inhabitants of Mars, Venus and Saturn and we may even greet the Jupterites. But he confesses that this wonderful science along geometrical lines, "Would come in conflict with orthodox and dogmatic religion." It is painful to think how many of us have been groping blindly and in darkness for many years under the delusion that the "Great Light" on our Altar reveal to us a merciful Father, the hope of immortal life and our duty to God and our neighbor, and have overlooked the great source of Truth revealed along Geometrical lines. Possibly we ought to replace the Holy Bible on our Altar with a copy of Euclid. But the author leaves a loop hole for our escape by saying farther along in his article: — "This is plain enough to one who is sufficiently interested and intelligent." I plead guilty to the last charge. These citations are given merely as an illustration of the kind of hysterical literature that is being written under the guise of Freemasonry.

But Hysteria is protean in its nature; it appears suddenly in unexpected quarters and under various disguises. Several years ago it broke out in the etymological field when a new prophet arose who contented that the words "Free Mason" are derived from the Egypto-Coptic language, and mean "Children of Light." This was a brand new discovery and from an unlooked-for source. Immediately the Masonic barns and woodsheds were filled with etymological gymnasts but they have merely rehearsed the old stunt without any additional thrills. Listen: "If we are to believe that our words, 'Free Mason' are derived from the ancient Egypto-Coptic language in which 'Phree' means light, knowledge, wisdom, or intelligence, while 'Messem' was the plural of 'Mes,' signifying children; hence we were originally known as children or son of light, wisdom and intelligence. Then, considering this, the true conception of the word 'Free Mason,' it will be seen that everything else is consistent, placing in evidence not only the spiritual and philosophical teachings of the Craft, but also showing the oriental origin and great antiquity of our beloved Order."

This is indeed a beautiful conception and we can only wish that Masons were children of the light, even if the etymology is very wabbly. The assertion that the words, Free Mason, are derived from the Egyto-Coptic language is another figment of fancy thrown out by "Repressed desire;" an effort to bolster up the flimsy claim that Freemasonry is founded upon the Egyptian mysteries. The facts are, there never was an Egypto-Coptic language. The Coptic language was spoken by the people of the Nile, until the Saracen conquest; it lives today only in Biblical literature, enriched with Greek and Hebrew words and embellished with a Greek culture of the Alexandrian School. The Egyptian language for the last twelve hundred years has been Arabic, and if there is or ever was a language known as Egypto-Coptic, it is a mongrel and not recognized by the best authorities.

The English language is made up of words derived from the divisions and subdivisions of the great Aryan Race whose root language is the Sanskrit. Upon this derivation, the etymology of the English language is based. The word "Free" can be traced back through the six or seven different languages to the Sanskrit root word, "Priya," the original meaning being beloved or dear. Through the different languages in which it can be traced it has its present meaning, "Free."

The word, "Light," comes from the Sanskrit word, "Ruch," meaning brightness. The root of this word is found in the language of all Nations, and means brightness or to shine. In the derivation of these two words can any one discover any relation whatever between the root "Priya" and the word "Ruch?" The wildest stretch of the imagination can not make them synonymous.

The claim that "Messem" is the plural of "Mes" will not bear investigation because in the Coptic Language the plural of a word ending in a consonant was formed by adding the letter "I," hence if the derivation were true it should be "Mesi," not "Messem." Judging from the spelling of the word Mason in the several centuries, the Egypto-Coptic word "Mes" had a difficult course to travel to find its imaginary plural. In the 16th Century the word was spelled "Maisson," "Masones" and "Maison." In 1611 we find the expression "Frie men of Maissones;" in 1634 it appears as "Frie Masones;" in 1636 it was written "Frie Mason." But not until 1725 was the Fraternity known as a "Society of Freemasons."

If the word Mason and the word Children, were ever synonymous we ought to be able to trace the root of these words. The word Child comes from the Sanskrit word *Ga* or *Gan* meaning "to beget." From this root word up through all the languages the word means child.

The word Mason can be traced back through all the prominent languages to the Sanscrit root, "Mit," which means to cut. Can any one find even a possible relation between the words meaning to be born, and to cut? Will any one claim that they are synonymous? Unfortunately for this fancy of "Repressed Desire," the lexicographers and etymologists are all on the other side of the question.

If "The spiritual and philosophical teachings of the Craft and the oriental origin and great antiquity of our beloved Order" depend on such flimsy and untenable arguments or hypotheses, then the Craft is in danger, both as to its teachings and its origin.

If any Mason wishes to draw geometrical figures and lines, and evolve from them that life continues beyond the grave, and to demonstrate the relation between the planets and the inhabitants thereof, no one will deprive him of the pleasure; but the Book on our Altar declared many Centuries ago that: "The Heavens declare the glory of God and the firmament showeth His handiwork. Day unto day uttereth speech and night unto night showeth knowledge." If any Mason wishes to amuse himself with the sacred triangles of Pythagoras, to demonstrate the unity of the world and the existence of Deity, well and good; but Freemasonry postulates the existence of God.

If any Mason enjoys himself by delving into the mysteries of Egypt and the Kabalah, no one will gainsay his zeal in his efforts to prove immortal life, the evidence of the spiritual world and the perfection of the Divine nature. It is well; but, Freemasonry accepts all this as axiomatic and concerning which there can be no denial.

Freemasonry is not a science of mental gyrations and abstractions, but it is the science of utilitarian thinking; it is not a philosophy of speculation, but it is the philosophy of doing; it is not a symbolism of Occult Sciences, but it is the mystery of the unfolding of a larger life; it is not so much as to origin, as it is to destiny; it is not so much as to the certainty of the past, as it is to the certainty and permanency in the future.

The liberal arts and sciences are worthy of every Mason's time and zeal, but these do not constitute Freemasonry. The ancestry of Freemasonry through the operative Craft is noble, the teachings of Freemasonry are sublime. Strained symbolism, abstract philosophy and etymological hypotheses add nothing to its luster, but rather dim its radiance in the broad field of practical morality.

Sentiment is the greatest thing in the world. Freemasonry is sentiment in action.

Geometry of God

Joseph Fort Newton

According to the measure of man, that is of the angel. Rev. 21:17

Few realize the service of the science of numbers to the faith of man in the morning of the world. It was almost his first hint of law and order in life when he sought to find some kind of key to the mighty maze of things. Living in the midst of change and seeming chance, he found in the laws of numbers a path by which to escape the awful sense of life as a series of accidents in the hands of a capricious Power. Surely it was not unnatural that a science whereby men obtained such glimpses of unity and order in the world should be sacred among them, imparting its form to their faith. Having revealed so much, numbers came to wear mystical meanings in a way quite alien to our prosaic habit of thinking— faith in our day having betaken itself to other symbols.

One of the first men to follow this hint was Pythagoras, of whom we know so little and would like to know so much. He was a lofty and noble figure, albeit half-hidden in myth, and only a few of his words have floated down to us. He saw in all the multiplicity of experience, to which Heraclitus had borne witness, a rhythmic march—a movement, but with disciplined step and the reasonable soul of music in it. One of his few sayings that remain sums up his vision: "All things are in numbers, the world is a living arithmetic in its development—a realized geometry in its repose." Take a snowflake and look at it under a glass, and you will see what filled that ancient thinker with wonder. It is an exquisite example of the geometry of God—squares, circles, triangles, pentagons, hexagons, parallelograms, more exact and delicate than the most talented hand could trace. Throw a stone into a still sheet of water, and immediately there arises an ever-widening series of concentric circles. The mountains in their strength stand fast forever, held in their places by a parallelogram of forces, and the stars swing round their vast orbits as noiselessly as a dewdrop is poised on a flower.

Such is the structure of the universe, and it is no wonder that Pythagoras saw in these signs and designs, everywhere present, the thought-forms of the Eternal Mind; else they would not be the natural, self-sought forms of matter. Nature is a realm of numbers, and the frolic architecture of a snowflake is a lesson in geometry. Music moves with measured step, using geometrical figures, and cannot free itself from numbers without dying away into discord. From Pythagoras this insight passed to Plato, whose opulent genius gave eloquent exposition to the Doctrine of Numbers. When asked by a pupil what God does, he replied, "God geometrizes continually," and he was often wont to say that Geometry, rightfully understood, is the knowledge of the Eternal. Over the porch of his Academy at Athens he inscribed the words, "Let no one who is ignorant of Geometry enter my doors," meaning that his teaching rested upon the science of numbers. What Plato and Pythagoras saw modern science confirms in myriad ways, as we may read, for example, in the researches of Henri Fabre. In the last chapter of his book on "The Cufic of the Spider," he wrote:

"Geometry, that is to say, the science of harmony in space, presides over everything. We find it in the arrangement of a fir-cone, as in the arrangement of an Epeira's living web; we find it in the spiral of a snail shell, in the chaplet of a spider's thread, and in the orbit of a planet; it is everywhere, as perfect in the world of atoms as in the world of immensities. And this universal geometry tells us of a Universal Geometrician, whose divine compass has measured all things."

How interesting it is, revealing the infinite ingenuity of the Divine imagination and the measured movements of its labors. Naturally we find hints of this science in the Bible, in which certain sacred numbers recur, indicating words, suggesting thoughts, and revealing truths. Nowhere is this more manifest than in the book of the Apocalypse, which, instead of being a series of clouded and confused visions, is a work of spiritual mathematics. In that book Three is the signature of Deity. Four indicates the world of created things. Seven denotes peace and covenant, while Ten is the symbol of completeness. Even numbers symbolize earthly things, odd numbers heavenly things, and the odd and even added unite the two. With this ancient science in mind, the vision of the City of God, with its geometrical design, takes a new meaning, albeit we should add to it the vision in the prophecy of Zachariah in which the young man is told that the holy city is not to be measured in cubits of human reckoning. Some hint of the paradox of the measurable and the immeasurable must have been in the mind of the Seer of Patmos, as if some one had asked him how our earthly cubits can form a calculus for that which knows not the gauge of time or space. Hence his parenthesis, to resolve the doubt, "according to the measure of man, that is, of the angel."

Man is a citizen of two worlds, but he has no skill to realize the world of spirit apart from the aid of the world of sense. If he asks, wistfully, about the life to come, the only answer is one expressed in the images and colors of the life that now is. As often as he tries to ponder, reverently, what is the essential nature of God, he finds himself thinking of the Eternal in terms of those moral qualities which he sees, dimly enough, in the noblest men. He cannot help himself; there is no other way for him to think. Truth, justice, mercy, goodness in man must be of the same nature as truth, justice and goodness in God, however they may differ in degree, else they mean nothing to us. Long ago Ovid said that "our measure is in our immortal souls," and our faith not less than our philosophy rest upon the fact that there is an angel in man, something akin to the Eternal, making our highest thought and vision valid. No doubt that was what Plato meant when he said that by the art of measurement the soul is saved — that is, by measuring up to the Angel within us we attain to the truth; by reading the reality of life through the highest, we learn its meaning and value. If so, we have our marching orders and the path of attainment is made plain even to the humblest, and no one need err therein or lose his way.

Just as in nature, from snowflake to star certain designs are found everywhere — circles, cubes, triangles — so, among all races and in all ages, certain ideas, ideals, faiths and hopes are held and trusted. Socrates made the discovery — one of the greatest ever made — that humanity is universal. By asking questions, which was the business of his life, he found that when men, whether they be artists or artisans, think round a problem and go to the bottom of it, they disclose a common nature and a common system of truth. After this manner the consensus of human insight, thought and experience confirms the fundamental truths of faith, like a problem of geometry, and we are justified in taking these basic ideas as the thought-forms of the Eternal Mind reflected in the mind of man. There is also a moral geometry which works itself out in the same way, tested by age-long and sorrowful human experience. Every evil way has been so often tried, that when we see a lad start along a dark path of evil doing we know what the result will be. No prophet is needed to predict the final issue; it is a problem in geometry. As David Swing said, in his noble sermon on "The Idealist," writing in his calm and simple manner:

"Some speak of ideals as if they were mere dreams. On the opposite all high ideals are only life-like portraits seen in advance. It would be much more true to affirm that ideals are the most accurate results reached by the most painstaking calculations. It stands much in their favor that they have come not from the brains of the wicked, but from the intellects that were the greatest. The greatest men of each age have pleaded for Liberty, because only the greatest minds can paint in advance the picture of a free people. Many nations are in the dust and mire today, because they have no minds great enough to grasp a divine ideal. Instead of being a romance, a noble ideal is often the long mathematical calculation of a mind as logical as Euclid. Idealism is not the musings of a visionary; it is the calm geometry of life."

For the rest, let us consider in a practical way the geometry of manhood, its proportions and dimensions. Like the Holy City, which the Seer saw descending from heaven, its length and breadth and height must be equal, as Phillips Brooks taught in his great sermon on "The Symmetry of Life," — which his church asked him to repeat ever so often. The basis of the triangle of character — that is to say, the length of a man, the extent of his influence and power, is a matter of morality. Purity is the first measure of a man. Lacking a certain simple, sturdy, homely moral quality, he is a man only by the accident of his shape, though he have the learning of Bacon, the grace of Chesterfield, and the eloquence of Webster. Morals are ever the boundaries of liberty and the primary dimensions of manhood. Honesty, purity, truthfulness — nothing can take their place, and without them religion is either a superstition or a sham. A pure heart may sanctify a creed, but a creed, however true it may be, must bear moral fruit before it can sanctify a life. To give morality any other than the first place is to invert the order of life and upset all its values. It is the foundation of character and of society.

But a man may be moral, and yet mean. He may be clean, but cruel; righteous, but uncharitable; truthful, and yet narrow, bigoted and hard. He may throw a poor family out of his house for lack of rent, and in so doing be honest—and inhuman! If there is anything worse than the wrongs wrought by wicked men, it is the evil done by good men. That which gives beauty, breadth and mellowness to life, melting our morality into goodness, is sympathy. And so to purity we must add pity. Justice runs lengthwise of life, but mercy is width, and is an evidence of nobility, of refinement, of graciousness of spirit. Lacking it, we have a Calvin in the church consenting to the death of Servetus because of a difference of dogma, and a Jaubert in fiction pursuing like a sleuth hound the weary, tangled and sorrowful steps of Jean Valjean. Man is akin to the animal, but God put into his heart an alabaster box of pity out of which, when once it is opened, come the amenities of life, its courtesies, its graces, and those extensions of sympathy which it is the mission of culture, not less than of religion, to promote. And tolerance, too, since heaven is only a village if it is made of only those thinkers who come always to the truth. Blessed be this broad and sunny sympathy in which bigotry and cynicism melt away and reveal to us the measure of man, that is of the angel that is in him.

There is yet another measure of manhood, what William James called "that altogether other dimension of existence," so often forgotten in our day. Some, to be sure, regard it as a kind of fourth dimension, a thing which you may argue exists, but which we can never realize. Not so. No Mason, at least, can think so. It is a natural, normal development of man, without which his life lacks symmetry and is a thing unfinished and imperfect. Call it a mystical faith, if you will, from it we derive most of our ideal impulses, our aspirations that transcend the merely sensible and understandable world. From beyond ourselves comes that ray of white light which can brighten the pale moonlight into a glowing sunlight, give to the light of the sun a sevenfold brightness, and glorify all common things—as De Hooge lets the sunlight fall on the rubbish of a back yard and wakens in us a thrill of joy and wonder.

Men must seek the heights of being, must be tall of soul as well as broad, if they are to see life in the large. Altitude of mind gives new proportions and perspectives, and shows that many things of which men are wont to make much are insignificant, and that other things, like a cup of cool water offered a Brother, are of eternal moment. It is when we add this third dimension that we see that men, when measured by the Angel in him, is immeasurable. Man is the measure of all things, said an ancient sage; but man himself, in the higher reaches of his being, cannot be measured. He is like an inlet of the sea. Looking landward, it is limited; looking seaward, it is linked with the infinite. "I think God's thoughts after him," said Kepler, as he looked through his glass into the sky, which is true of all high human thinking, all noble living, all upwardleaping aspiration. Truly, He that made us hath set eternity in our hearts, and restless we are until we find our rest in reunion with His will in which is our peace.

Let us strive, then, to unite purity, pity and prayer in our lives, revealing the length and breadth and height of life. Also, let us judge life and our fellows by the Ideal of the Angel, that so, at last, when we are tested by the measure of the Angel—that is, by the Angel of Death—we may be found to have attained, in some degree, to the measure of the stature of true manhood. And by as much as we have failed, by so much let us trust the mercy of God which is without measure and knows no end—

> *For the love of God is broader*
> *Than the measure of man's mind;*
> *And the heart of the Eternal*
> *Is most wonderfully kind.*

The Suppression of the Order of the Temple
Frederick W. Hamilton

Circumstances have conspired to single out the Order of the Temple from the other orders of Soldier-Monks of the twelfth century for the particular notice of succeeding generations. Preeminent for their valor and their accomplishments during the days of their magnificent success, the bitter injustice and cruel suffering attendant upon the suppression of the Order has thrown around their name a dark shadow of tragedy. Not only so, but the added horror of the accusations made against them, the whispers of still more dreadful things circulated by envious, fearful, or malignant tongues, the unusual end of the proceedings against the Order, and the conviction of many members before the ecclesiastical courts have lent an air of mystery to the whole sad story.

The very mention of the word Templar brings to many minds the suggestion of romance and of mystery coupled with a vague sense of hidden crime and lurking horror. As a matter of fact there is really very little mystery about the fate of the Templars and it is perfectly possible to find out of what they were accused and to make a fair estimate of their probable guilt or innocence. This is of particular interest to Masons because large numbers of Masons in other than symbolic degrees have taken the name of the old Order, endeavoring to practice its principles and emulate its virtues and holding in everlasting remembrance the name of the last Grand Master.

Before proceeding to tell in detail the story of the fall of the Order, let us stop to review briefly the story of its growth.

In 1118, two Knights, Hugues de Payens, a Burgundian, and Godeffroi de St. Omer, a Frenchman, associated with themselves six other Knights for the service of the Holy Sepulcher, the protection of pilgrims, and the welfare of the Church.

These men took a step beyond that taken by the ordinary crusader, in that they undertook to give their whole lives to the service of the Church militant and to found an order of men likewise devoted to the same service. These eight men took an oath to the Patriarch of Jerusalem by which they swore to fight for Christ under the three fold vow of poverty, chastity, and obedience. It will be understood, of course, that the vow of poverty, while it debarred the Knight from having any personal possessions whatever, did not apply to the accumulation of riches by the Order or to the Knight's enjoyment of those riches, while the vow of obedience had reference only to his relations with his superiors in the Order.

King Baldwin I. of Jerusalem gave them for a residence a part of his palace next to the Mosque of Aksa, the so-called Temple of Solomon, from which they took the name of Knights of the Temple. At first they had no particular regulations or "rule," as it is commonly called, and no distinguishing dress. Their first idea appears to have been to make the Order a means of reformation by opening its ranks to men whose past was one of sin and failure and giving them an opportunity to redeem their souls through offering to Christ a service of constant danger. They, therefore, admitted to their number excommunicated knights, after they had obtained absolution from a Bishop, and other men of darkened past who desired an opportunity to bring forth fruits meet for repentance. This missionary idea was soon abandoned and the Knights chosen from candidates, who showed themselves worthy. It was unfortunate, however, in that it immediately laid the Order under suspicion of both the Church and laity because of doubts of the sincerity of such repentance.

In 1127, Hugues de Payens, who had been chosen Grand Master, went to Europe with the purpose of finding support for the Order. He was fortunate enough to enlist the interest and obtain the active patronage of St. Bernard. Bernard of Clairvaux, more commonly known as St. Bernard, was the greatest and most influential churchman of his time and one of the greatest of all times. Under his patronage the Order quickly obtained favor and support and grew in members and power.

St. Bernard drew up the "rule" or series of regulations governing the organization of the Order and the lives of its members. The original "rule" of St. Bernard was written in French. Unfortunately there are no early copies of it known to be in existence. There are however, later copies together with the translation into Latin known as the "Latin Rule" and additional statutes which were adopted from time to time.

It was vehemently asserted by the enemies of the Order, in later years, that there was a secret "rule" quite different from this which entirely changed the character of the Order, colored it with heresy, and stained it with sin. There is no evidence whatever that any such "secret rule" ever existed. Stories about it may be safely dismissed as idle gossip.

The French "rule" provided for the officers of the organization and defined their duties. It also carefully regulated the daily conduct of the Knights and provided for the support which they should receive from the common funds of the Order. It is interesting to observe that the "rule" provided that each Knight should have three horses and one squire. By favor of his commander, or prior, he might have four horses and two squires.

This effectually disposes of the legend that the great seal of the Order, representing two Knights mounted on one horse, was intended to indicate that in early days the Order was so poor that the Knights went to battle mounted thus in pairs. The second rider in the device is probably intended to represent either a wounded Knight who is being rescued by his brother in arms or a pilgrim being protected by a Knight of the Temple.

The Knights were not priests. That is to say, although under the three vows they were not in holy orders. Each priory or house of the Knights was provided with one or more chaplains. These chaplains were members of the Order of the Temple and were always in holy orders. The chaplains were exempt from ordinary ecclesiastical jurisdiction. Spiritually they were accountable only to the Pope; temporally only to the Grand Master. They were the sole confessors of the Knights, who were not permitted to accept the ministrations of religion from any but their own chaplains unless it was impossible to secure a chaplain's services.

The monastic custom of having the Bible read at meals was prescribed by the "rule" for the Knights, in consideration of the fact that they were laymen, and consequently uneducated, the Bible was read in the vernacular and not in the Latin which was customary in religious services. There is in existence an old French Bible of the Templars which shows evidences of the critical spirit on the part of the translator.

With this brief survey let us pass on to the opening years of the fourteenth century. The little band of eight Knights sworn to the service of the Holy Sepulcher and the protection of pilgrims had grown to be one of the great powers of the world. If its purpose and policy had been other than they were it might have shaken the power of any monarch in Christendom. It consisted of many thousand Knights besides the lay brothers and feudal servants of the Order. It possessed wealth far greater than that of any state in Christendom. This wealth was the result of the great stream of gifts which for two centuries had flowed steadily into the coffers of the Order, supplemented by the spoils of war, and coupled with great financial ability. Kings, princes, and nobles throughout Europe had vied with each other in their great donations to the Order of the Temple. It owned literally thousands of estates all over Europe and wherever in the east the crusades had been successful.

The crusades being over and their immense expenditures having ceased, the enormous revenues of the Order were accumulating in its hands, and those were not idle hands, for the Templars were not content to let their gold pieces lie idly in their treasury. This was before the age of modern banking and the Templars, with their great wealth, their many establishments, and their connection with the Orient, made themselves the great international financiers of the age. Kings and merchants alike borrowed on good security and at ample interest the unused treasure of the Order. Oriental exchange, especially, was almost absolutely in their hands so that they acted as the great financial clearing house between Europe and Asia. Their establishment, commonly known as the Temple, at Paris was the center of the world's money market.

It is said that when De Molay came from the east, lured by the treacherous call to consult about the crusade, he brought with him 150,000 florins in gold and ten horse loads of silver. With due allowance to the difference in the purchasing power of money, the gold was probably the equivalent of three million dollars today. I have no way to guess the value of the silver, but it must have been very great. This, it will be remembered, was the ready money upon which De Molay could lay his hands at short notice.

The power of the Order matched its wealth. The Grand Master was a sovereign prince, recognized as a full peer of any monarch in Europe. The Knights, save those too old for warfare, were all soldiers trained to arms and owing no allegiance to any power but the Grand Master and the Pope. During the stormy years of the crusades, they, with the Knights of the companion Orders, formed the fighting edge of the Christian army. Combined with their lay brothers and the feudal array of their tenants they formed an army far superior to any other in existence.

That an Order possessed of such wealth and power should have been regarded with suspicion, and even fear, is only natural. It is entirely clear, however, from their entire history, and especially from their fate, that the Order had no policy in the political affairs of Europe either for its own advantage or that of any others. The Knights adhered strictly to the original policy of the Order. They had no enemies in Christendom and no friends outside of it. Their sole military and political purpose was the service of the church and the reconquest of the Holy Land. It must be remembered that while we know that the crusades were over in 1300 the men of that day did not know it. They fully expected that the crusades would be resumed, and the Knights of the Temple were maintaining their numbers and diligently increasing their wealth in order to be able to strike more effectively than ever before when the banner of the Cross should once more take the field against the Crescent.

In addition to all their wealth and power the Order had great privileges of two classes, lay and clerical. As lay nobles they held and exercised all the usual feudal rights in and over estates which had been given to them, with certain extremely important additions. The Order, being a corporation in the first rank of the feudal hierarchy, exercised what was known in those days as high, middle, and low justices, that is, complete jurisdiction extending even to the infliction of the death penalty. Owing allegiance only to the head of their Order, the estates of the Knights were not liable for military service except to the Order itself. The estates of the Order were the permanent possessions of the corporation.

The greater part of the revenue of the kings of that age was derived from certain rights of taxation which were exercised on special occasions; for example, the passage of an estate by death or marriage from one holder to another involved certain payments to the king or overlord which amounted practically to an inheritance tax. The marriage of children, the knighting of the noble's sons, or other events in the family of the noble were occasions for gifts to the king which were practically taxes. Other forms of taxation were laid from time to time on the feudal estates. But corporations do not die, do not marry, and do not have children, consequently the estates of the

Templars were free from every kind of taxation, except for the benefit of the Temple itself.

This exemption from military service and from financial burdens struck at the very roots of the royal power as the state was organized in the middle ages. The Templars enjoyed all the benefits of the feudal system but bore none of its burdens. When an estate in France or England, for some reason, passed into the hands of the Templars it was to all intents and purposes taken out of the kingdom as effectively as if it had been swallowed up by the sea.

As an Order of military monks, the Knights enjoyed clerical privileges equally great.

That their spiritual affairs were in the hands of their chaplains, has already been pointed out. In addition to this, the Grand Master and others of the high officers possessed the power of disciplinary confession, but not of sacramental confession, a point important to be remembered in connection with later developments. The Order as a whole and its members individually were entirely free from the jurisdiction of bishops and other ecclesiastical authorities. They were accountable only to the Pope in person. They were not affected by general censures or decrees of the Pope unless they were especially mentioned. Their churches, of which there were great numbers on their various estates besides those attached to their houses, were not affected by ordinary excommunication and interdicts. No matter what ecclesiastical censures might hang over the people of the nation the activities of the churches of the Temple went on undisturbed. Excommunicated persons might be buried in consecrated ground belonging to the Templars, and this was not infrequently done. They possessed, by papal decree, the right to have churches not their own which were under interdict opened twice a year and services held for the purpose of presenting their cause and taking collections for the support of the Holy War. They collected the usual tithes from the churches on their estates but they did not pay any tithes, even for those churches, into the coffers of the Church.

The natural result of this condition was envy and hatred on the part of both civil and religious authorities. Civil authorities looked on with dismay while the broad lands of noble after noble passed by gift or bequest into the control of the Templars and ceased to contribute to the maintenance of the state, while the individual noble was filled with envy as he saw the Knights of the Temple enjoying privileges and powers so much greater than his own, and the law officers of the crown indignantly found their authority everywhere terminating at the boundary line of one of the Temple estates.

On the other hand the religious authorities, accustomed to control the lives and actions even of kings, were enraged beyond measure to find themselves utterly powerless before the Knights of the Temple. Entrenched behind the many privileges granted by a long line of Popes the Templar could and did snap his fingers in the face of the most arrogant archbishop or cardinal and the angry churchmen had to swallow his wrath and digest it as best he could, while he had not even the poor consolation of collecting revenues from the parishes in his jurisdiction which had passed into the hands of the Order. This sort of thing had raised tides of envy and hatred against the Order of which it seemed to be strangely unconscious.

Claims that the Knights abused their power and privileges were common. The picture of the Templar in Scott's Ivanhoe undoubtedly represents the widespread conception of the character and conduct of the members of the Order. That there were men like Scott's Templar could hardly be denied, but there is no reason to believe that they were typical of the Order generally.

One feature of the Order gave the opportunity for proceedings against it and the excuse for its undoing. The Order of the Temple was always a secret order. Its conclaves for business and for the reception of candidates were always closely guarded. It was as impossible for one not a member of the Order to get into meeting of the Knights of that day as it would be for like person to get into a meeting of one of our modern gatherings of Knights Templars.

This secrecy, as is inevitable, in all ages and especially in times of ignorance and superstition, like the thirteenth and fourteenth centuries, bred all manner of suspicion. Men, and especially ignorant men, are ready to believe that evil things are done in places where they are not admitted and unfortunately there were too many who envied and hated the Templars and were ready to spread these whispered accusations. It was asserted that under cover of this secrecy the Knights not only lapsed into heresy and consorted with Saracens and other misbelievers but that they practiced idolatry and necromancy, that they performed the most blasphemous travesties of religion, and that they were given to licentiousness and practiced every conceivable crime, natural and unnatural.

We have now set the stage for the tragedy. Let us consider a little the persons and antecedents of the three principal actors. They were the Grand Master of the Templars, the King of France, and the Pope.

The Grand Master of the Templars, who had in been office since 1295, was Jacques de Molay. He was a simple, unlettered Knight, personally brave, confiding and unsuspicious, incapable of intrigue or treachery, not very clear headed or resourceful in the face of other than physical peril. His intentions were always good; his conduct under the severe trials to which he was subjected was sometimes weak. He was a man who could be easily deceived and could be worked upon through his reverence for the Pope, his respect for the King, and his honest desire to protect the interest of the Order and the welfare of his brother Knights.

The Knights generally were fighters and some of them were men of affairs, but they were not thinkers and they were not intriguers. It has been said that they were too stupid to be heretics but this is probably an extreme statement. They were rather simple minded single hearted gentlemen thoroughly loyal to the cause to which they had dedicated their lives and for which they were ready to die.

The King of France was Philip IV, commonly known as Philippe Le Bel or Philip the Fair, a name, by the way, which would better be translated, Philip the Handsome. Born in 1268 he ascended the throne in 1285. As his name indicates, he was a man of singular beauty, being said to be the handsomest man of his time. He was cold, self-contained, farsighted, crafty, and unscrupulous. He possessed great ability and was absolutely remorseless in the choice of means and in the pursuit of his ends. It is said that he was never known to smile and those whom he crushed in the cold persistency with which he executed his purposes said that he was not a man at all, but that his beautiful body was inhabited by a demon instead of a human soul.

It must be admitted that from the point of view of the interests and prosperity of the kingdom he was a good king. In his day France was well governed and strongly consolidated and he left it on the whole in a much better condition than he found it. He had one supreme end in life and that was to make the royal government supreme in France. He was determined that the government should be independent of priests or noble and the king should have a free hand, not limited in the exercise of his authority by any powers within or without the confines of the kingdom.

To accomplish this he believed that two things were necessary. One was that the shackles imposed by the papacy upon the King of France, in common with the other monarchs of Europe, should be broken and the crown of France relieved from the domination of the Vatican. The other was that the feudal nobles should be brought into subjection to the crown and especially that the independent power of the Order of the Temple should be broken, their wealth plundered for the filling of the royal Treasury, their great estates restored to the usual condition of feudal dependency, and their resources of men and money made available for the purposes of the kingdom.

The Pope was Clement V. In order to understand the conduct of Pope Clement, it is necessary to go back a little. At a comparatively early period in the reign of Philip, Boniface VIII ascended the throne, in 1294. The predecessor of Boniface was Celestine V, one of the most singular popes who ever occupied the chair of St. Peter.

Deeply imbued with mysticism, he was a dreamer of dreams and a writer of strange books. The sanctity of his life and the strangeness of his somewhat unintelligible writings placed him on the narrow edge between condemnation as a heretic on one side and canonization as a saint on the other. Whether saint or heretic, he was utterly unfit for the difficult administrative duties of the papacy. He never wanted to be Pope and after a short and troubled reign he was induced to resign, and sought seclusion, which was really imprisonment, in a monastery, where he died in a very short time.

Boniface was certainly the leader in the movement which brought about the resignation of Celestine and was charged with being the author of the unfortunate old man's misfortune. At any rate, he succeeded him on the papal throne. There was quite a good deal of doubt in the minds of canon lawyers as to whether a pope could resign, and therefore a cloud rested on the title of Boniface, a cloud which was only partially dispelled by the death of Celestine. The enemies of Boniface, and he had many, declared that the death of his predecessor was not a natural one and that Boniface himself was responsible for it.

Boniface was proud, arrogant, and rash. He declared himself overlord of all the monarchs of the world, and set the high water mark of papal pretension. On one memorable occasion, when there was a vacancy in the office of Emperor, the Pope appeared in public, brandishing his sword and declaring that he was Emperor as well as Pope. He claimed, and attempted to exercise, power to set up and pull down kings and even emperors.

Naturally, Philip the Fair and Boniface very soon found themselves engaged in a deadly conflict. Boniface laid France under an interdict and excommunicated King Philip and his family. The King, supported by a host of the clergy as well as the laity of France, appealed to a future Council of the Church. It is worthy of mention that this appeal was signed by the Order of the Temple. The appeal struck Boniface in his most sensitive spot. The question of whether or not a Council was superior to a Pope had not yet been settled and the assumption that it was his superior was unspeakably exasperating to the overbearing, tyrannical Boniface.

King Philip was far too aggressive to content himself with this appeal. Seizing an occasion when the pope was absent from Rome on a visit to Anagni, his native town, and comparatively undefended, the king sent his chancellor, William de Nogaret, and Sciarra Colonna, a great Italian noble who was on bad terms with the pope, to arrest Boniface. By whom Philip expected that the pope would or could be tried is not clear. The charges preferred were intrusion, that is to say, forcing himself into the papal chair without proper title, gross immorality, tyranny and heresy.

Boniface was actually arrested and treated with great indignity. Some authorities say that he was actually struck in the face by Colonna. The people of Anagni rose and overpowered the guard and released Boniface, but the shock of his arrest with the attendant humiliation and indignation caused his death within a few days.

He was succeeded by a somewhat colorless pope, Benedict II, who ruled only from October 27, 1303, to the seventh of the following July. He released France from the interdict and Philip and his family from excommunication, but his reign was otherwise unimportant.

Now came the question of the election of a new pope, in which Philip proposed to play an important part. His attention fell upon Bertrand de Got (Gouth). De Got came from a Gascon family and was an Aquitainian, that is to say, an English subject, for it must be remembered that at this time about half of what is now France belonged to the dominions of the English kings, either by descent from the Dukes of Normandy, or by virtue of the marriage of Eleanor of Aquitaine to Henry III.

De Got was Archbishop of Bordeaux. He had been an early friend of Philip, who knew the man thoroughly, but in the quarrel between Philip and the pope, he had sided with Boniface. Election to the papacy was not then limited to the cardinals, and the Archbishop of Bordeaux might well aspire to the tiara. He was extremely ambitious, hungering with all his soul for wealth, honor, and power. Philip knew his man and believed that as pope he might be controlled, especially if he was made to feel that he owed his election to the king.

Philip did not see the Archbishop personally, as has been claimed by many writers, but he did unquestionably have an understanding with him through intermediaries before using his influence to secure his election. Two questions were raised by King Philip. One was the question of the suppression of the Order of the Temple, for the interest of both church and state through the abolition of the power and privileges which made the Templars so objectionable to both. The other was the question of the heresy of Boniface VIII. King Philip threatened to bring pressure to bear which would make it necessary to call a General Council before which he would impeach the late Pope of heresy. In view of the great unpopularity of Boniface and of certain things said and done by him, there appeared to be great danger that the charge could be pushed home and the memory of the late Pope tainted of heresy to the great scandal of the church and disgrace of the papacy.

De Got was unscrupulous enough to agree to almost anything in order to be made Pope and he therefore agreed to co-operate in the suppression of the Order of the Temple if the king would agree not to press the charge of heresy against his predecessor. With this understanding King Philip supported his candidacy and he was elected Pope and took the title of Clement V.

As might be expected it very soon appeared that Bertrand De Got who wanted to be Pope and Clement V who was Pope, were not quite the same person. Like many another successful politician before and since the Pope had no intention of fulfilling pre-election promises if he could get out of it.

His first movement was to propose the consolidation of the Order of the Temple with the Order of the Hospitalers. This would then enable him to reorganize both bodies and amend their charters.

This project was proposed in 1306, but was abandoned on account of the vigorous opposition of the Grand Masters of both the Orders. The Pope then proposed to reform the Order of the Temple, but moved slowly in carrying out the project.

King Philip was very impatient at the Pope's delay and continually pressed him to fulfill his promises of suppression under threat of a general Council and condemnation of Boniface VIII for heresy. He was not content, however, with insistence and threats. Through his agents he found two broken Knights of worthless character, Esquiau (Squin) De Florian, a Frenchman, and Noffo Dei (Deghi), a Florentine. These men claimed to have been members of the Order of the Temple and offered pretended confessions in which they charged the Order with heresy and various abominable practices. For all this they were well paid.

On the basis of this manufactured evidence Philip submitted formal charges to the Pope. The Pope received them, but continued to delay action. Philip's determination, however, was more than a match for the Pope's procrastination. He found means to force the Pope's hand through the intervention of William of Paris, Grand Inquisitor of France. The Grand Inquisitor had been King Philip's confessor and was entirely ready to lend himself to the King's desires. By virtue of his office he had power to take summary action in all cases of heresy within the kingdom and to take such measures as he saw fit to deal with them.

Philip submitted his evidence to the Grand Institor who forthwith demanded of the civil authorities the arrest of all the Templars in France. Obviously this was a very serious matter. If the Templars had taken concerted action to resist such an arrest it would probably have been impossible. Assembled in their strong houses they might have stood siege until aid could have reached them from other countries and it would have been a very serious question whether Philip could have retained his throne. Plans were therefore laid for their capture by surprise and arrangements were made for the simultaneous arrest of all the Knights throughout the kingdom on the night of October 13, 1307.

The blow came like lightning from a clear sky. It is true that the Templars had been aware of the circulation of unpleasant reports. They knew that there were whispers of evil and De Molay had gone as far as to ask, in 1306, that an investigation be made into the conduct of the Order, but investigation was the last thing the King desired and no attention was paid to the request.

The apprehensions of the Templars were set at rest and their confidence was further deliberately strengthened by the treacherous conduct of the King. In 1306 King Philip had been assailed by a mob in the streets of Paris and saved himself from great personal danger by taking refuge in the house of the Templars which happened to be not far from the scene of disturbance. This obligation, however, rested lightly on his conscience. The Templars were accustomed to have a public reception of Knights in addition to the private initiation and King Philip attended such a public reception the spring of 1307. On October 12, the very day before that fixed for the arrest, De Molay was present by invitation, at the funeral of King Philip's sister-in-law and was assigned a place of honor among the participants in the ceremonies. It is not to be wondered at that the blow of October 13 was an entire surprise and was entirely successful. De Molay and all the Knights in the kingdom were arrested, their goods were seized, and their houses taken possession of, without the slightest attempt at resistance so far as we have any record.

The events which ensued are somewhat complicated and consist of two distinct sets of proceedings, first, personal proceedings against the individual Knights and second, proceedings against the Order as a whole and in all its branches.

Proceedings against the Knights were the first in time. They were begun with great vigor by the Grand Inquisitor of France, but there was some question about the Grand Inquisitor's jurisdiction. Particular rights and immunities of the Templars which have already been noted might be considered as placing them beyond the reach of proceedings not instigated by the Pope, or at least approved by him.

The Grand Inquisitor, however, would not allow himself to be troubled by questions of this sort and immediately proceeded to examine the arrested Knights under torture.

We must not forget that this was not an unusual proceeding. The examination of accused persons, and even of witnesses, under torture was the ordinary method of judicial procedure at that time. It was not a method confined to the Inquisition but was commonly practiced by the civil courts. It would have been very unusual if it had been omitted in this case. Horrible as it appears to us and useless as a method of ascertaining the truth, it was an every day occurrence in the 14th century and was absolutely relied upon as a method of getting at facts.

Torture was not confined to physical torment. The accused were promised clemency if they freely confessed the acts with which they were charged and named their accomplices. In the case of the Templars such promises were conveyed in letters under the royal seal. These letters were decoys pure and simple. They were either forgeries or deliberately written with intent to deceive and without the slightest intention of keeping the promises which they contained.

The accused were told that if they retracted these confessions they would suffer the pains of death in this world and of hell in the world to come. It was realized that men under physical torture will often say almost anything which may be suggested to them as a means of securing relief from their sufferings and these means were taken to prevent a retraction of these forced confessions.

Moreover the law of evidence in use in those days contained one provision which seems to us a peculiarly ghastly mockery. The confessions which were wrung from the lips of the tortured victims were taken down as uttered. Depositions thus obtained were taken to the victim after he had recovered from the first effects of the torture and he was asked to sign them. If he did thus sign them, aware that a refusal to do so would mean renewal of the tortures together with the before mentioned threats of death and damnation, confessions thus signed were held to be voluntary and not legally made under torture.

Naturally many of the Knights confessed. De Molay himself made a partial confession. Most of these confessions were afterwards retracted, but for the time being they stood.

The charges will be examined further on, but the principal things confessed should be noted here. They were:

Denial of Christ. Defiling the Cross by spitting upon it and by other methods too indecent to describe.

Indecent kisses which it was claimed the initiates were compelled to give the receiving officer on various parts of his body.

Sodomy. This, by the way, was a vice much more common in the 13th century than now and was ordinarily a part of any serious accusations made against either individuals or groups of individuals. It was one of the charges against Boniface VIII when he was arrested by De Nogaret and Colonna.

Idolatry. This was based on the alleged worship of an idol, of which we shall hear more, and on the accusation that the cord which was part of the habit of every Templar was consecrated by this idol by being touched to it before the Templars put it on. Other abominations were vaguely referred to but these were the main points of the accusation.

De Molay confessed only to spitting on the cross, denying the other allegations. He seems to have been led to this partial confession, which in a way was an evidence of weakness, by several considerations. One was fear of torture. Although De Molay appears to have been a man of personal courage in the battle field and was capable of dying a painful death with heroic resignation, as we shall see later, he seems to have shrunk from the threat of torture. He was also promised clemency if he would confess and he appears to have believed that a partial confession would open the door to freedom and enable him not only to save himself, but the other Knights. We must remember that De Molay throughout was conscious of his responsibility as Grand Master, and in all his actions he appears to have felt that he must consider not only himself but the brethren of the Order who were under his command. He also feared a definite charge of sodomy aimed against himself. There is no reason to believe that there was a slightest proof for such a charge but De Molay's enemies were active, ingenius, and unscrupulous. They had manufactured a case against him and they had witnesses ready to sustain the charge by perjured testimony. In those days escape was difficult if the tribunal desired to convict and there is little doubt that if De Molay had been tried upon this charge he would have been convicted. No matter how unjust such a conviction, it would have meant death and dishonor. It is no wonder that De Molay was not willing to face this. Under these circumstances he made his confession, but he declared that he would offer satisfactory explanation if only he could be allowed to submit it in person to the King or the Pope. What this explanation probably was we shall see later. It is needless to say, however, that De Molay was not permitted to make it, and his confession was held by his enemies for all it was worth and more.

When Pope Clement heard of these proceedings he was extremely angry. He immediately issued an edict suspending the Grand Inquisitor, and sent a committee of cardinals to investigate and report. Unfortunately, however, the case had gone too far to be stopped, as the King perfectly well knew. Individuals might be punished, but in some way or another proceedings would have to go on. Philip was not in the least daunted by the Pope's anger or disturbed by his interference. He arranged for a conference between himself and Clement which was held in June, 1308. The King, who, throughout these proceedings shows himself to have been much the stronger personality of the two, took the aggressive by demanding of the Pope five extremely unpalatable things.

    1. Canonization of Celestine V.

    2. Condemnation of Boniface VIII for heresy.

    3. A general Council to take into comprehensive consideration the affairs of the Church.

    4. Papal absolution for De Nogaret.

    5. Removal of the papacy from Rome to Avignon.

Clement yielded with regard to the canonization of Celestine, the absolution of De Nogaret, and the removal of the papacy. This was the beginning of the long residence of the popes at Avignon which is known in history as the "Babylonish Captivity." The condemnation of Boniface and the general Council were two things to which he was entirely unwilling to consent. In return for the relinquishment of these points he did exactly what Philip had foreseen and desired; he abandoned the defense of the Templars.

After considerable negotiation a bargain was struck between the Pope and the King. Two sets of terms were agreed upon, one to be made public but not to bind either the Pope or the King, the other to be kept secret but to be regarded as binding. According to the first, which was a tissue of treacherous falsehoods, the Templars were to be taken from the French-authorities and placed in the hands of the Pope as representing the Church. The property of the Order was to be held in trust by the Church and the proceeds were to be used for carrying on the crusade; that is to say for the purpose for which it was originally intended. The suspension of the Grand Inquisitor and others who had been involved with him was to be removed. The terms of the private agreement were far different. The Church, on the plea that it had no facilities for the care of so large a number of prisoners, was to leave the persons of the Templars in the hands of the King. The property, instead of being held and administered by the Church, in trust, was to be held by Philip on behalf of the Church and was to be administered by a Board of Administrators, half of whom were to be appointed by the Pope and the other half secretly appointed by King Philip. In other words, the Templars and their goods were handed over to the tender mercies of the King. Such was the price in humiliation and dishonor which Clement paid for the title of Successor of St. Peter.

The next act in this tragedy was the summoning of a Council to try the Order as a whole. Henceforth here were two processes simultaneously going on, one against the Knights as individuals and one against the Order as a corporation. This gave opportunity for more treachery.

As we have seen, the King had played the game with loaded dice from the beginning and now the dice were loaded even more heavily than ever, if such a thing were possible. A net was spread from which it was well nigh impossible for any one to escape, while the proceedings were extended to other countries. It is not necessary to go into the details of the story of the proceedings outside France. In a general way, so far as the individual Knights were concerned, they were similar to the French proceedings although conducted with varying degrees of severity according to the temper of the several monarchs who were concerned in the matter. Actions against the Order as a whole were covered by the proceedings which we are about to trace.

Knights were summoned from far and near to come to the defense of the Order in its hour of trial. They were asked by the papal authorities to come and speak in its defense and they naturally understood that this implied personal immunity. They soon found, however, that nothing of the sort was intended. When each Knight appeared he was asked if he desired to defend the Order. If he said that he did he was immediately made a defendant, not only in the process against the Order but in the personal process against the Knights. If he took alarm and said that he did not wish to defend the Order, he was held as a witness, liable to examination under torture.

Many Knights, trusting to their immunity as witnesses, withdrew their former confessions which, as will be remembered, were obtained under torture. They withdrew these confessions because they were false and because they desired to defend the Order as a whole against the charges to which they had personally pleaded guilty under compulsion. Considerable numbers of those who withdrew their confessions in this way were immediately burned as relapsed heretics. This, by the way, was the ordinary procedure in those days in the case of dealings with heresy. As a rule there was very little chance for the accused to escape. If he refused to confess he was convicted and burned on the testimony of others. If he confessed and withdrew his confession he was burned as a relapsed heretic. If he confessed and did not withdraw the confession, he was burned as a confessed heretic. About the only difference was that in the last case he received absolution, which was supposed to save his soul, and was sometimes able to save his property for his family. Moreover, not content with the ordinary partiality of judicial proceedings in those days, the two sets of proceedings were made to play into each other and evidence obtained in either trial was used indiscriminately against the defendants in both.

Interest centers largely around the tragic figure of De Molay. As we have already seen, he had been examined by the Grand Inquisitor in 1306 and had made a partial confession. He was kept in close confinement although he demanded an opportunity to appear before the Pope who, it will be remembered, was the only person in Christendom to whom he owed allegiance, and submit to him an explanation of the acts with which he was charged.

In 1308 he was visited by three cardinals sent by the Pope. He was solemnly assured that he was now in the hands of the Church, from whose clemency and aversion to cruelty and bloodshed everything favorable could be expected. He was promised mercy by both the Pope and the King on the strength of a full and free confession. He renewed his confession, although he did not extend its scope, and threw himself on the mercy of the Church. He was given absolution by the cardinals, was restored to the communion of the Church, and was actually given the sacrament by the cardinals. This was distinctly stated by the cardinals in a report which they made to the Pope.

In spite of all these facts, however, he was not set at liberty, though he vigorously demanded it and urged the fulfillment of the promises which had been made to him.

In November, 1309, De Molay was brought before the Council which was trying the Order. Being asked if he would defend the Order he refused to plead. He appealed to the Pope, pleading the rights of the Order and demanding to be heard by the Pope in person. In response to the charge of idolatry he made solemn affirmation of orthodoxy. Being charged by De Nogaret with having dealings with the Saracens contrary to his vows and to the interests of Christendom, he said that the alleged dealings consisted only of truces and treaties made with them as incidents of warfare and for the sake of saving the Christians in the Orient from disaster. The charge of sodomy was brought up, but was not pressed with much vigor and the prosecution failed to establish it by even plausible testimony. De Molay then demanded to be set at liberty, claiming the failure of the accusations and the promises of both the Pope and the King. The request, however, was denied and he was sent back to his dungeon.

The tedious proceedings against the Order dragged on for three years. Every effort was made to suppress the defense and to discourage or destroy the defendants of the Order. Again and again the chosen representatives of groups of Knights were either executed or silenced. Executions continually took place as the result of the other set of proceedings and care was taken that these executions should be as damaging as possible to the defense of the Order.

The proceedings lasted until May 6, 1312, when the Pope, by a summary exercise of his authority, dissolved the Order. It is important to note that the Order was never condemned. The proceedings against the Order were never finished. While they were still going on the Pope intervened and put a stop to the proceedings and to the Order at the same time. Examination of the evidence shows that the charges were not substantiated, at least in any way which would appear to satisfy modern ideas. It is quite probable, however, that had the proceedings been allowed to come to their natural end the Order would have been condemned. It is difficult to see how the Pope and King could have permitted the proceedings to come to any other conclusion.

The intervention of the Pope was for the particular purpose of saving the immense properties of the Order for the Church. By the law of that day the property of a condemned heretic passed not to the Church but to the State. If the Order of the Temple had been condemned for heresy its immense possessions would have passed to the rulers of the countries in which they were located and the Church would not have touched a penny. Dissolution of the Order, however, without condemnation threw its numerous properties, scattered over Europe and the east, into the hands of the Church. Pope Clement was not so sincere a defender of orthodoxy that he had the slightest intention of taking all his trouble for the purpose of enriching Philip of France and other kings of Europe. He preferred to let the Order go uncondemned, to leave the Knights to the tender mercies of kings and inquisitors, and to save the money for the Church.

In this, however, he was only partially successful. It will be remembered that in France, at least, the King was the custodian of the property of the Templars and he succeeded in keeping a very large part of it. The same thing happened to a greater or less extent in the other countries. The Pope, however, succeeded in getting a portion of the wealth into his possession and a considerable part of this finally found its way into the hands of the Hospitalers. It is not to be understood that the Hospitalers were participants in the proceedings against the Templars. The Order of the Hospitalers was the greatest militant Order of Knights in existence except the Templars and the natural administrator of property given in trust for the crusades.

De Molay remained in prison until December, 1313, when he was brought before three French cardinals. The old vague promises of mercy were made and De Molay once more renewed the old confession again without extending its scope. He was taken back to his dungeon and told that at a certain time the cardinals would make their final decision in the case. Trusting to the repeated promises which had been made, De Molay came before them on March 10, 1314, expecting liberation, probably accompanied by heavy penance and possibly other penalties. To his amazement he was sentenced to life imprisonment. De Molay, it will be remembered, had been in prison for seven years. Whether he had been actually tortured or not is not quite certain, but imprisonment itself was torture in those days and De Molay was not willing to face the prospect of a further imprisonment which could terminate only in his death. He was shocked, angry, and broken hearted at the treachery which he had met at the hands of both State and Church. As soon as the sentence was announced, De Molay arose in his place and retracted his confession, declaring that it was not true, that he had confessed only out of willingness to please the King and the Pope and a desire to help his brethren, and that he now wished to withdraw his confession, proclaim its untruth, and take the consequences. The cardinals, in confusion, adjourned their court until the next day. This was something entirely unexpected and they desired time to think it over.

King Philip, however, had no intention of allowing his prey to escape him or of giving the cardinals the desired opportunity for meditation. That very night De Molay was taken from his prison by a detachment of the King's guards and burned at the stake on a little island in the Seine. In spite of the high-handedness of these proceedings, involving the invasion of the rights of the Church by taking its prisoner from its hands and putting him to death, the cardinals did not dare to raise a word of protest, so great was the ascendancy which the King had obtained over the Pope. It is stated by tradition that when De Molay went to the stake, he solemnly summoned the Pope and the King to meet him before the bar of eternal justice within one year. Whether or not this legend is true, it is true that within the year Clement and Philip were both in their graves.

Whether for good or evil the Order of the Temple was suppressed forever. No other body of men ever enjoyed such wealth, such power, such privileges, and such immunities as had been enjoyed by the Templars. Whether they had used them wisely or not, it is not always easy to say. That they were in a very real sense injurious to both State and Church, we shall probably all agree. That the Templars did not deserve so cruel a fate as that which overtook them seems clearly established. In order to make this point clear, let us make a brief examination of the indictment drawn against the Order and the probable truth, or lack of it, in the charges.

The indictment against the Order contained 117 articles, or counts as we should style them. This great number of counts was partly the result of technical repetitions. In many cases the same accusations were repeated in different forms, the first charging that a specified offense was committed by all of the Knights, the second that it was committed by most of them, and the third that it was committed by some of them.

Stripped of verbiage and repetition the charges came down to the following:

Denial of Christ.
Defiling the Cross.
Requiring indecent kisses from the candidates.
Denial of the sacrament of the altar.
Omission of the most significant words from the mass.

Granting of absolution for sins, even when not confessed, by the Grand Master.

Exacting an oath never to leave the Order.

Holding secret conclaves.

Permission to the members to practice sodomy.

Actual practice of sodomy.

Worship of Idols.

Adoration of a cat.

Use of cords which had been touched to an idol.

Murder of candidates for refusing to take the oath of secrecy

Murder of members for revealing the secrets of the Order.

Confession only within the limits of the Order and not to outside priests.

Failure to correct or reveal the evils which the members of the Order knew to exist.

Failure to discharge the duties of hospitality which were incumbent upon the Order.

Covetousness and rapacity in obtaining possession of the property of others.

The indictment closed by alleging the confessions which we have already considered as proof of the truth of the charges.

It would be tedious, perhaps, to examine the charges in detail, but a few of them should have careful consideration.

We know that the conclaves of the Order were held in secret and that no outsiders were admitted to their ceremonies. That was not a crime, but it was a cause of suspicion.

We have no sufficient evidence either that candidates were murdered for refusing to take the oath or that members were murdered for revealing the secrets. In this respect, as in some others, the agitation reminds us of the anti-Masonic charges of a later time and especially of those connected with the name of Morgan. Fundamentally the same human characteristics are involved.

Charges of immorality are certainly not substantiated by the evidence. That there were immoral individuals in the Order could hardly be denied. It would be impossible that so large a body of men should be free from unworthy members. It would be rash to deny that there were individual cases of sodomy. The crime was common in the middle ages and has always been the curse of celibate communities. That it was particularly common among the Templars or sufficiently common to blacken the fame of the whole Order is absolutely without proof. Indeed there is very little evidence in the trial bearing at all upon this point.

The charge that the practice was permitted finds absolutely its only shadow of foundation in the fact that a section of the "rule" provides that when there were not sufficient accommodations for each Knight to have a separate bed, two might occupy the same bed rather than that one should lie upon the floor.

The charge of covetousness and rapacity is natural. When a rich noble died and left all his property to the Order his heirs, naturally enough, were not particularly pleased. They doubtless had a good deal to say about undue influence and other things which we hear about today. That the action of the Order was particularly objectionable in this respect does not appear from the evidence.

The charge of parsimony and lack of hospitality was abundantly refuted.

The charge of heresy or the holding of forbidden beliefs was not proved and was always denied by the Knights.

The omission of significant words from the mass or any other form of blasphemy was not only unproved but was vigorously denied by practically all of the witnesses. The charges relating to heresy are denied not only by the testimony of the witnesses but by the entire history of the Order. It is extremely probable that the cosmopolitan character of the Order and the contact of its members with men of many nationalities and of different faiths had the inevitable result of broadening their views and giving them a certain toleration and largeness of personal outlook. It is very difficult for a man who comes constantly in contact with all sorts and conditions of men and with a great number of national and racial types to continue a fanatic. During the whole course of their existence, however, the Knights were the foremost to shed their blood and spend their lives for the Christian faith, that is to say for orthodox Catholicism. They were the cutting edge of the crusading armies, rivaled in this regard only by the Hospitalers. Again and again detachments of the Knights were cut down to the last man fighting for the cross and refusing to surrender to the infidel or even to flee from him. Men do not show such determination as this for a faith in which they do not believe.

As for the matter of confession and absolution. We know that the rule of the Order especially provided that the members should have their own chaplains, to whom they should make their confessions when it was possible to do so. This rule was drawn up by St. Bernard and approved by the Pope. Obedience to it on the part of the Knights could hardly be considered a crime. It was abundantly proved that the Grand Master did not give ecclesiastical absolution. He did have the right to receive disciplinary confessions, to condone offenses against the Order, or to inflict disciplinary penance. This was a purely administrative matter and had nothing to do with clerical absolution. No Grand Master ever presumed to give clerical absolution.

The charge of idolatry arose from a curious misapprehension. It was alleged that the Templars worshiped a brazen head. This head, it was said, had a white beard and rested upon a tall tripod. To this head the Templars were said to pray, and it was charged that the cords which they wore as a part of their habits were consecrated to it by being touched to it. The great church of the Templars in Paris possessed a very sacred relic. It was said to be the head of one of the 11,000 virgins who were martyred with St. Ursula at Cologne. It is interesting to know, by the way, that the legend of the 11,000 virgins rests upon a misreading of an old Roman inscription. The inscription tells of "XI M Virgines." M was read as an abbreviation for "mille" but it was really the abbreviation for "martyres" and instead of being read 11,000 virgins it should have been read 11 virgin martyrs. However, the head in question was believed to be the head of one of the virgins, whether there were eleven or eleven thousand. This head was covered with a white linen cloth and was covered again by a gold or bronze case in the shape of a head. When the case was slipped over the head the linen cloth showed at the base of it. The relic was displayed on special occasions before the high altar of the church, mounted on a tripod. This was the bearded, brazen head which the Templars were said to worship. There were probably reproductions of this reliquary in other Temple churches. It is probable that the Templars were glad to consecrate their cords by touching them to this sacred relic as was a common practice in those days.

The charge that indecent kisses were required is probably true, though not as a universal practice. This appears from a considerable number of depositions. This was done probably from one or both of two reasons. It may have been required as a test of obedience. It will be remembered that the Knight swore the three great vows of poverty, chastity, and obedience. Obedience was held to be absolute. Once the Knight had sworn he was under this bond and was bound to do without question anything that he was told to do by his knightly superior. His obedience was immediately tested by this requirement. The second reason is almost unintelligible today but is perfectly intelligible to anyone who is familiar with the life and habits of the middle ages. It was a rough joke, and it was the kind of thing that the medieval mind considered funny. Wit and humor as we know them were very rare in the middle ages. Their places were taken by unspeakable coarseness. Anyone who is familiar with the art, literature, and drama of the middle ages is only too familiar with this fact. The more filthy and indecent the story or incident the more it appealed to the rough humor of the time and the louder the laugh which it excited. Contrasts of rough buffoonery with the most solemn incidents appealed to the minds of the people of that age. It was only in accord with the habits of the time that after the solemn ceremonies of the initiation the candidates should be subjected to a bit of foolish buffoonery.

There remains the charge of denial of Christ and defiling the cross. That there was any denial beyond the alleged defilement of the cross does not appear. That the candidates were sometimes, not always, commanded to spit upon the cross or otherwise defile it was confessed by De Molay and seems to be clearly established by other testimony. It will be remembered, however, that De Molay insisted that he could explain the fact, and the explanation appears in the testimony of some of the witnesses. Witnesses usually testified that they did not spit upon the cross but upon the ground near the cross, and some of them testified that when commanded to do so they refused. Those who refused were congratulated upon their courage and told that they would certainly be good soldiers of the cross. In other words the command to defile the cross was a test. The candidate having sworn obedience and having sworn to serve as a defender of the cross was immediately put to the most difficult and trying of all tests, a test which involved conflict of obligations. He was called upon to choose whether he would fulfill his vow of obedience at the expense of his vow of loyalty to the cross, or whether he would carry his loyalty to the cross so far as to break his oath of obedience. It must be remembered that this was an age in which obedience was a virtue and that the efficiency of the Order, or any similar body, depended upon the absolute obedience of its members to the orders which they received. As has already been pointed out the loyalty of the Order to the cross is written in blood on every page of its history, whatever may have occurred at the initiation. Undoubtedly the explanation De Molay would have made, if he had been given opportunity to do it, was the one just indicated, that this ceremonial requirement was a test and entirely void of any deeper significance.

A survey of the charges and the evidence seems to show that the condemnation of the Templars was an act of great injustice and that the suppression of the Order was certainly not warranted by the charges which were brought against it. That the privileges and immunities of the Order worked to the weakening of the state, the impairment of the king's power and authority, the injury of the Church, and the lessening of the authority of the bishops, must be clear to anyone. That both Pope and King breathed easier after the Order had ceased to exist is entirely probable, but that its crimes were such as to deserve the treatment it received certainly does not appear from any facts in our possession or brought out at the trial.

One question will at once arise in the minds of every Mason, "Did the Order survive its suppression and is there any direct connection between the ancient Templars and modern Templar Freemasonry?"

So far as we have any evidence this question must be answered in the negative. Legend states that De Molay appointed a successor and a line of Grand Masters is named connecting the ancient and modern Orders. De Molay had no right to appoint a successor. The election of Grand Master is carefully provided for in the rule of the Order and no provision is made for any other form of procedure under any circumstances. There is no evidence whatever for the authenticity of the list which is sometimes given.

Some of the Templars who survived joined other orders and some of them passed their remaining days in obscurity or imprisonment. There is no traceable connection between the ancient Knights of the Temple and any modern order. The most we can say is that it is possible that the traditions and even the secrets of the Order were cherished by its surviving members after the Order was dissolved. Men do not easily forget things which have been very dear to them, for which they have suffered, and for which they have seen their companions die. That there was any esoteric rule or belief among the Templars, we have no evidence. That there was a certain freedom of thought and breadth of view would be the inevitable result of that cosmopolitanism and contact with the outside world of which we have taken account. It may be that the survivors of the Order, hoping against hope that it might some day revive, may have communicated their hopes, their aspirations, their ritual, their views, and their secrets, if such there were, to their chosen friends and in this way the soul of the Order may have survived until it reappeared in other forms, and its ideas and ideals may have been influential some centuries later in the development of those movements which resulted in the transformation of Masonry from its old operative into its modern speculative form. But all this lies in the field of conjecture. As far as the sober historian can see the Order of the Temple ceased with the edict of May 6, 1312, which absolved the Order, and the tragedy of March 10, 1314, which ended the life of De Molay.

A Masonic Lesson from a Raindrop
Charles N. Mikels

The Sun was created a long time before it was even partially understood. Those who were blind thought that its purpose was to "dispense light." Much was said about light. Somebody learned that Sahara was a desert and yet had an ocean of light. The desert lacked something practical.

Then people conceived the idea that maybe the Sun had more than one purpose; that it made heat and power; that heat and power were necessary to make light serviceable; that heat made raindrops and raindrops made power.

Unintelligent observation nearly spoiled the reputation of the Sun. He seemed to many, to peep over the horizon simply to flirt with the wavelets of the sea. He stimulated them until they were ready to fly to pieces. He called them pet names in vibrations so rapid that human ear could not register them. The wavelets wanted something genuinely hot. They wanted to get near something which had a burning heart. Finally the sea submitted to a change of form and part became something better. The sea vaporized and the vapor aspired to the Sun.

This Maker of Light caused a never-ending modification of conventional water. The vapor climbed on steps of air until it obscured the light of the Sun itself. Then it received "a new name" and was called a Cloud.

Even the clouds are misunderstood. They drift and drift until they strike against a cold and fruitless mountain top. The immovable mountain could not understand a change. The cloud meant to softly caress the mountain and moisten its dry brow, but there was no welcome. The clouds were chilled. This drifting dust of the sea shrank and crowded together in sensitiveness; centralized in sympathy; had no real helpfulness until it did centralize. A raindrop fell as a result.

The cloud died in giving birth to a raindrop. While it fell, a sunbeam from the heart of the Sun, shot into the raindrop, ran around its walls, saw that it was an improvement over the sea and came out a rainbow of Hope with a message of Change. It seems odd that God cannot be satisfied with things as they are but must put on a policy of change. Even a rainbow changed sunbeam.

Crazy with disappointment, the raindrop started down the mountainside, homesick for the sea. It traveled in foreign countries. It dodged around boulders which hindered its progress. No immovable "forms" could stop it. It saw other homesick raindrops and "joined" them in a common purpose. Enough of them form a tricklet, a streamlet, a rivulet, a river, yet a river is nothing but a few million heartsick raindrops sprinting for their cradle in the sea.

A raindrop has a "rough and rugged road to travel from the mountain top of yesterday to the sea of tomorrow. It is little but it is mighty. It is slow, but is persistent. Harness a raindrop to the horns of Gravitation and it will dig a canyon. But what use has the world for a canyon, a big gash in the bosom of earth, which has to be bridged or stop travel? A canyon is a purposeless, brainless, heartless monument to waste energy until you make another change.

Fraternalize a raindrop, a grain of sand and a changed sea shell and you can dam a canyon which is an unused opportunity. Then you can turn the canyon's liquid energies into heat and light and power. You have to add head and heart and hand to do it. You put the hoe of purpose into the hands of intelligent method under the direction of common-sense and imagination, to get a new result out of old forces in a new way.

Twin raindrops as alike as two peas, did two things. One acted conventionally and caused waste. The other sprung an innovation and warmed the world.

There is a lodge room on the banks of the Niagara River, in which to learn many mysteries. Its covering is a clouded canopy or starry-decked Heaven. Many have paid an initiation fee in car fare and hotel bills to visit it. A few people "work" there. A few return. The great majority of initiates never come back. All wear an indistinct memory as a badge of membership.

The Falls are one of the mysteries of God. Many have admired its age. Some have been awed with its tireless voice of Omnipotence. Others marvelled at its unmastered might. Generally people had no practical purpose when they went there and had none when they left. The river was nothing but raindrops and the Falls were nothing but a jump of raindrops which could not wait.

After the centuries had grown weary with waiting for God to tell some man what is the great mystery of the Falls, an innovator stood on the same spot and saw the same sights. The waste challenged his wit and opened his heart. God whispered to him that the Falls were meant to be used, and not looked at merely. Wonderful, age-old mystery! Practice, and not theory!

This spectator talked about changing the situation. Every sightseer who had no ideas, called him crazy. This particular spectator decided that God created Niagara River and Niagara Falls for a practical purpose; that the purpose had never been seen or had been forgotten; that God never meant waste of time or opportunity or power.

In his sincere simplicity this unconventional, unsophisticated soul had heard of people who said often and far and wide, that the thing they most desired was "light," "more light," "further light." He thought that they meant it, but they didn't; they merely wanted to talk about wanting it. There it was running away, enough to answer their wildest dreams and not a soul would permit the answer to their own wishes because it came in a new way. They did not see the end from the beginning. They had no imagination. They did not know how. The idea was too big for them to grasp easily and at once.

This sightseer was obsessed by the thought that he had a wireless message from God; that he alone understood the situation. He suggested that some of these Niagara raindrops be diverted to practical uses instead of stereopticon views.

What a storm of indignation broke upon his head! Change is never practical in prospect. An established change is a habit. The Falls were perfect as they were. Let well enough alone. They are as they were yesterday. That is good enough for tomorrow. He was laughed at but the laugh did not take. He fought first to get the world used to the idea. It did get used to his thought. Nothing can head off, permanently, the reign of a sound idea.

This fellow, who was of no official importance, argued that a practical engineer should dream out the details of a practical plan to cause raindrops to manufacture and deliver light and to deliver heat and power with light. He argued for a constructive instead of a "stand pat" policy. He argued that men with burning hearts should replace men who sit on the brakes of progress. He argued for a central light plant instead of the raindrop system. Everybody said that there could be none, because there had been none. But there was.

What difference did it make to this innovator that the President, Senators, Congressmen, Governors, Legislatures, all the officiary of habit, were against him! What difference did it make because those who want ideas digested and fed to them as if they were young mental robins, insisted on sleeping in comparative darkness, on the brink of a good thing! It was his business to wake them. He was talking about the purposes of God. God wanted the world to actually and really have more light, heat and power.

The world did not care what God wanted. People wanted that to which they were accustomed. The bottomless canyon of habit intervened. Niagara Falls had always been "an ancient landmark" of waste, and waste is a virtue when it is old enough.

People of petrified purposes fought him, doubted him, hindered him. The dynamic heart of this custodian of God's purposes of helpfulness, hammered the idea into the heads of men for their own good. He literally hammered, repeated, reiterated until he forged the key of attention which opened the door to their brain cells so that an idea could walk in. He aroused interest; study followed; purpose ripened; judgment acquiesced; some assisted. Everybody knows what happened. The right was permitted to prove that it was right. The right prevailed. The logic of efficiency conquered. The raindrops were commanded to turn aside. They co-ordinated for the benefit of man. These sovereign, independent raindrops were organized and directed by a combination of masterful intelligences possessed of a combined purpose.

More light and heat and power followed. Everybody is used to the idea today, hence it is safe. Men of those days shied at this practical idea of helpfulness just as western broncos shy at a stray page from the Bible. The bronco does not understand the Bible. He never tried. If he knew anything he knew that the usual place for a page of the Bible is in a property room of a Church, home or Lodge. An active page from the Bible in a strange place has to be explained to men even.

God has plenty of time to wait and he has plenty of patience. Man has but three score and ten years so he has to be in a hurry to see ideas bud, blossom and bear fruit. The persistence of this dreamer of innovations, made him a pest to all whose heads were asleep.

And yet all but this dreamer were mistaken. It did not hurt the world nor mar Niagara Falls to change its purpose and plans.

There was less light when these raindrops had no leadership. Light is applied theory. It is intelligent practice. Heat is not frenzied fancy. It is useful every day and not merely on Saturday night on or before full moon. Power is not fiction. It is fact, helpful fact. It is sane to secure more light, to secure aggressive heat, to increase power by change.

With the potential power of a river of God's, Masonry has rambled and twisted through the bed of two speculative centuries without the direction of organized premeditation. To change the figure, it has plowed a great furrow in history. But it never had a headplowman who knew anything about intensive farming.

Masonry has stood pat in the face of God's manifest policy of evolution, and has prided herself on the fact. It even glories in repeating words, phrases, paragraphs, degrees which have lost their fitness like the Fellow Craft's degree.

Four or five times in these centuries, some incarnation of Fortitude, has dared to challenge the perfection of Masonry just as Preston did. He was an innovator. He was a Masonic heretic demanding the light of education. He made a change, a radical change, a helpful change. We are used to his change now, so we forgive him, we applaud him. New styles in thoughts, ideas, practice and purposes are no more popular than new shoes. Maybe the shoes will not fit. When soles wear out, you have to get new ones or go to bed and sleep.

Preston jarred the brain cells of his co-temporaries. He compelled them to think. He compelled them to think when they did not wish to think, of things with regard to which they did not wish to think. So did Krause, Oliver and Pike. They should have been expelled as disturbers of the age-old peace. Why in the world, did they not let well enough alone? Wasn't Masonry growing in numbers fast enough; collecting initiation fees enough, wearing badges enough, building enough Temples ? What more could you want ! Practical purposes of the heart are less easily understood than practical purposes of dollars.

Your National Masonic Research Society isn't an innovation. No one need to be afraid. You have simply jumped back one hundred and fifty years to get a little of the purposes of Preston. You have resurrected a part of a dead purpose. He talked of education in general. You talk of Masonic education in particular. This purpose is narrow enough to be safe. Certainly you are safe. God is probably applauding you while we fear lest you let the logic of Truth guide you fearlessly, no matter where it takes you. You might find out what God meant Masonry to do and be and how.

You cannot prevent our learning at least one thing from Preston, Krause, Oliver and Pike. They slipped the straight jacket of habit from their minds and hearts. They proved that there is a mental peace which is stagnation.

Masonry has an unpremeditated and unspeakable responsibility because it has permitted nearly 2,000,000 men in this country alone, to pass its ritualistic doors. If Masonic Truth is being eagerly, frequently, heartily, personally incorporated in the lives of 90 per cent of these members, under the direction of Grand Masters, Past Grand Masters and Grand Lodge Officers, Masonry is a practical, vitally effective fraternal order and these officers should be crowned with "Well done."

If you have to drum up quorums, apologize for lack of attendance and interest when degree work is done, if scarcely 10 per cent of the 2,000,000 members get under the influence of Masonry at all, there is a lack of heat and power at least.

Sovereign raindrops running independently through a channel of habit, without real purpose, without practical plans, without power, without head, call for another of God's inspired changes.

Runaway raindrops are an emblem of waste. Waste is inefficiency. Masonry is a progressive science if there is progress. Does it fit the modern heart or is there a lot of lost motion? Is Masonry efficient? Could it be made better? Can you make it better? Will you make it better? How?

The first thing to do is to get your Masonic bearings. Understand it as it is. Is Masonry efficient?

Was William Shakespeare a Freemason?
Robert I. Clegg

A few pertinent paragraphs from the great Bard, bearing on words and phrases in common use among the Craft:

"Put on two leather jerkins and aprons." -2 Henry IV., 2: 190.

"They will put on two of your jerkins and aprons." -2 Henry IV., II, 4:18.

"Here, Robin, an I die, I give thee my apron." -2 Henry VI., II, 3:75.

"The nobility think scorn to go in leather aprons." -2 Henry VI., II, 2:14.

"Hold up, you sluts, your aprons mountant." -Timothy of Athens, IV, 3:135.

"A carpenter – where is thy leather apron and thy rule?" - Julius Caesar I, 1:7.

"Mechanic slaves with greasy aprons, rules and hammers." - Antony and Cleopatra, V, 2:210.

"He will line your apron with gold." -Pericles, IV, 6:64.

"You have made good work, you and your apron." - Coriolanus, IV, 6:96.

"Being then appointed Master of this design." -Tempest, I, 2:163.

"The singing Masons, building roofs of gold." -Henry V., I, 2:98.

"What is he that builds stronger than either Mason?" - Henry V., I, 47.

"Who builds stronger than the Mason?" -Henry V., I, 57.

"Creaking my shoes on plain Masonry." -All's Well That Ends Well, II, 1:31.

"You shall see him in the triple pillar of the world." -Antony and Cleopatra, I, 1:12.

"And set it down with gold on lasting pillars." -Tempest, V, 1 :208.

"And call them pillars that will stand to us." - 3 Henry VI., II, 3:87.

"He is not our Craft's Master." -2 Henry IV., III, 2 :297.

"Wooing poor craftsmen." -Richard II., I, 4:28.

The above very interesting compilation appeared in the March, 1918, issue of the *Rob Morris Bulletin*, the bright publication of Rob Morris Lodge, Denver, Colorado, and is of course the production of its able editor, Henry F. Evans. One cannot but wish that our excellent brother had had the space and time to elaborate his article at such length and skill as his sound Masonic knowledge and literary capacity fully warranted. Then indeed we should have the more nearly arrived at a solution of the really knotty question behind the references he has patiently assembled and which but whet our curiosity to a keener edge. There is no present intention to offer a complete answer to the query. At the best we can but carry forward the inquiry a short stage or two but we shall feel quite content if we attract attention to the problem.

We are also denied the satisfaction of going thoroughly and definitely into explanations. This cannot be done in print. The reader must read between the lines. He must make his own references. If his remembrance of ritual is hazy and incomplete there is but one remedy, get the co-operation of some well-informed Mason, or better still, take the article over to the lodge and read it to the brethren. Their reaction will help. There is wisdom in the counsel of many.

Neither shall we on the present occasion delve into the peculiarities, political or otherwise, of the Elizabethan era. We have pointed out on another opportunity the Craft relation of the gilds and their pageantry and we shall curb our temptation to go deeply into Shakespeare's acquaintance with the trades and their customs. To take but the single instance, William Blades has put on record so many allusions to the one trade, printing, that Shakespeare might from the testimony of his literary output be set down not unfairly as an exponent of that calling.

How much did he know of Freemasonry ? We may perhaps meet the inquiry by submitting such evidence as shows what he knew of things and of practices that especially concern Freemasons. Obviously these can be but fragmentary and merely suggestive.

Clarence tells us of King Edward's mysticism in these terms:

"Hearkens after prophecies and dreams;
And from the cross-row plucks the letter G."
- Richard III, I, 1.

One might infer that the allusion is to some means of divination, forecasting the future, as the term "cross-row" is to be found explained as meaning the alphabet. Sometimes the alphabet was accompanied with a cross in the old primers or was arranged in the form of a cross as a token of good luck. But the choice of the letter "G" is significant.

Falstaff's death gives in a word by Mistress Quickly, "chrisom child," "Henry V.," II, 3, a striking comparison. Knowing the fullness of the reference the Freemason can with Shakespeare see the larger vision. For the child when christened was given a white garment and anointed with oil, the while was said the following prayer, "Receive this white, pure and holy vestment, which thou shalt wear before the tribunal of our Lord Jesus Christ, that thou mayest inherit eternal life. Amen." After the member of the Craft has thought over the Apron lectures of Brothers Strobo and Shaver, and also conned over the color allusion by Stowe, "Chronicles of London," to the gifts of the godfathers of "christening shirts with little bands and cuffs, wrought either with silk or blue thread," he will see no doubt what Shakespeare saw, the dying of an old man like unto an innocent child, as one wearing and deserving the purity badge of an Entered Apprentice, "went away an it had been any chrisom child."

Praise to excess is often spoken of as if it were laid on with a trowel. So does Shakespeare speak of it with reference to that very working tool of the Craft, see "As You Like It," I, 2.

Our friend and brother, the great Pythagoras, was by no means unknown to Shakespeare who mentions him by name and alludes familiarly to the theories associated with his school of philosophy. For example:

> "To hold opinion with Pythagoras
> That souls of animals infuse themselves
> Into the trunks of men."
> - Merchant of Venice, IV, 1.

Another instance is in "Twelfth Night," IV, 2:

> "What is the opinion of Pythagoras concerning wild fowl?"
> "That the soul of our grandam might haply inhabit a bird."

Transmigration of souls is elsewhere mentioned by Shakespeare, as in the "Tempest," IV, 1, and in "Hamlet," IV, 5. That beautiful if fanciful -certainly not unscientific-idea, "the music of the spheres," was also Pythagorian and well-known to Shakespeare. Thus it is said in the "Merchant of Venice," V, 1,

> *"There's not the smallest orb which thou beholdest,*
> *But in his motion like an angel sings."*

Does Shakespeare allude to the North? Yes, he deems it the place of darkness and of evil. He mentions a devil assigned to the north. The spirits, "I Henry VI.," V, 3, are sought "Under the lordly monarch of the north." See also "I Henry IV.," II, 4, and the "Merry Wives of Windsor," II, 2.

There is a noteworthy passage in "King John," IV, 2:

> *"And when they talk of him they shake their heads*
> *And whisper one another in the ear;*
> *And he that speaks doth gripe the hearer's wrist,*
> *Whilst he that hears makes fearful action,*
> *With wrinkled brows, with nods, with rolling eyes."*

The sight of the open hand, as in the outstretched hand when extending it to clasp that of a presumed friendly acquaintance or raising the hand when taking an oath in a court of law or elsewhere or when elevating the hand in giving a military salute or answering one, all these and similar acts had a wider meaning in the days of Shakespeare than is even now known to many of the profane. Then it was not uncommon to brand criminals or otherwise maim or mutilate them. The word "stigma" means such an effect as if burned deeply by fire. Just as the mutilated criminal showed that those in authority had branded him noticeably to the end that the beholders could never mistake him for one unrestrained and unrestricted, free of birth and will, so the person born deformed or accidently so was deemed thus crippled or defaced by the will of God to designate his evil nature. Accordingly in "Richard III.," I, 8, the hunchbacked Duke is called:

> *"Thou elfish-marked, abortive, rooting hog!*

Thou that was sealed in thy nativity,
The slave of nature, and the son of hell."

Bacon, about the same period, and by the way we will not here venture into a discussion of the true authorship of the plays of Shakespeare, but Bacon refers to the deformity of the body accompanying a perversion of the mind. Thus, agrees Shakespeare,

"A fellow by the hand of nature mark'd,
Quoted, and signed, to do a deed of shame."
- King John, n, 2.

"And the blots of nature's hand
Shall not in their issue stand;
Never mole, hare-lip, nor scar,
Nor mark prodigious, such as are
Despised in infancy."
- Midsummer Night's Dream, V, 1.

"But thou art neither like thy sire nor dam;
But like a foul misshapen stigmatic
Mark'd by the destinies to be avoided
As venom toads, or lizards' dreadful stings."
- 3 Henry VI., II, 2.

Probably an allusion to the branding by a heated crown is indicated by the words in "Richard III.," IV, 1. Assuredly there is some ground for the belief that some regicides, notably the Earl of Athol executed for the murder of James I. of Scotland, were tortured with a circlet of hot iron around the head. Note the passage:

"O, would to God that the inclusive verge
Of golden metal, that must round my brow,
Were red-hot steel, to sear me to the brain."

There is a classic story of the tree that revealed to Aeneas the murder of Polydorus in discovering the grave of the one so patiently sought. The account is to be found in Virgil or Dryden's translation of that author, III, 22. Shakespeare seems quite familiar with it. Thus in

"Macbeth," III, 4, referring lo the fact that murder will out, we are told,

> "*It will have blood; they say, blood will have blood;*
> *Stones have been known to move, and trees to speak;*
> *Augurs and understood relations have*
> *By magot-pies and choughs and rocks brought forth*
> *The secret'st man of blood.*"

The symbolism of the glove is all but lost among Freemasons, not so in the days of Shakespeare. There was a time when the giving of a pair of gloves to the newly-made Mason was as significant as was the bestowal of anything else. Not infrequently a second pair of gloves was given the new member to be in turn transmitted to the one he loved best of the opposite sex. Today the Freemason is mainly accustomed to the white gloves as an appropriate emblem of mourning to be worn at a Masonic funeral or as adding a touch of Masonic uniform or "clothing" at any other ceremonial of a public character. Shakespeare refers to the gloves as a favor to be exchanged freely by friends but when once acquired and worn it could only be demanded as the act of an enemy. For instance,

> "*Give me any gage of thine, and I will wear it in my bonnet; then if*
> *ever thou darest acknowledge it, I will make it my quarrel.*"
> "*Here's my glove; give me another of thine.*"
> "*There.*"
> "*This will I also wear in my cap; if ever thou come to me and say,*
> *after tomorrow, 'This is my glove,' by this hand, I will take thee a box on the*
> *ear.*"
> - Henry V., IV, 1.

Appropriately enough from a Masonic point of view where the glove has equal weight with the apron in symbolism, Shakespeare calls it "honor's pawn," and a "token of honor," as may be seen by an examination of "Richard II.," I, 1; "Richard II.," IV, 1; "Timon of Athens," V, 4.

We are taught as Masons that the form of a lodge is oblong; its length from east to west, in breadth from north to south, as high as heaven, and as deep as from the surface to the center. Thus are we shown the universality of Freemasonry and that a Mason's charity should be equally extensive. But the expressions must sound strange to the young Freemason, much more strange than they would have been to the ears of Shakespeare. He uses east to west in the same limitless fashion thus:

"O heaven, that such companions thou'ldst unfold,
And put in every honest hand a whip
To lash the rascals naked through the world
Even from the east to the west!"
- Othello, IV, 2.

And as to the center, pray consider the following,

"As true as steel, as plantage to the moon,
As sun to day, as turtle to her mate,
As iron to adamant, as earth to the center."
- Troilus and Cressida, III, 2.

There is also the claim of the self-confident Polonius who says,

"I will find
Where truth is hid, though it were hid indeed
Within the center."
- Hamlet, II, 2.

While dealing to some extent with the points of the compass we must not overlook the location of graves upon which there is an interesting note in Tylor's "Primitive Culture," vol. 2, page 423. He says,

"It is not to late and isolated fancy, but to the carrying on of ancient and widespread solar ideas, that we trace the well known legend that the body of Christ was laid with the head toward the west, thus looking eastward, and the Christian usage of digging graves east and west, which prevailed through medieval times, and is not yet forgotten."

He also quotes an old work to the effect that the laying of the head to the west was for the purpose that the dead should rise looking toward the east. Did Shakespeare know of this centuries-old belief ? He did, as may be seen from the following, relative to the burial of the dead,

'*Nay, Cadwal, we must lay his head to the east;*
My father has a reason for't."
- Cymbeline, IV, 2.

On many occasions we have called attention to the punishment by drowning, the tying of the culprit to a stake at low water and then leaving the body there for at least the period of a couple of tides. Around this old English treatment of criminals grew up certain expressions and superstitions of the liveliest interest to we Freemasons. They are duly noted by Shakespeare. Thus of a rascal in the "Tempest," I, 1, it is said,

"*Would thou might'st lie drowning*
The washing of ten tides."

And in the "Midsummer Night's Dream," III, 2, we find,

"*Damned spirits all,*
That in cross-ways and floods have burial."

Falstaff's death is said to have been

"*Even at the turning o' the tide.*"
- Henry V., II, 3.

and in the passing of the king in "2 Henry IV.," 4, is thus recorded by Shakespeare,

"*The river hath thrice flow'd, no ebb between;*
And the old folk, times doting chronicles,
Say it did so a little time before
That our great grandsire, Edward sick'd and died."

Of symbolism we have a wealth of references, too many for easy selection. In mere allusion to numbers there is too large a choice as the mention of significant numerals is extensive. Threes, sevens and nines are noted as of special importance by Shakespeare, as truly they are to all Freemasons. In fact he has put into the mouth of Falstaff, "Merry Wives of Windsor," V, 1, an explanation with which we may conclude this compilation,

> *"They say there is divinity in odd numbers,*
> *Either in nativity, chance or death."*

Of the symbolism of numbers much is taught in Freemasonry. Three, five, seven, nine, and their multiples are frequently met. All have a pertinent significance for the persevering student of the message shown and conveyed by symbolism. Among the manifold references it is well to reread in this connection the information to be found in the Mackey-Hughan Encyclopedia, Hastings' Dictionary of the Bible (the article on "Number"), and Morals and Dogma (pages 548 et seq).

Was Shakespeare aware of the peculiar associations that these particular numbers have for many if indeed not all of us ? It is very likely that he was so informed. The obvious fact that these numbers are uneven was not unnoticed by him. Nay, he goes further and speaks of odd numbers in a way indicating his acquaintance with the beliefs that had grown around them through the ages of mankind's infancy and mental growth. Thus,

> *"They say there is a divinity in odd numbers, either in*
> *nativity,-chance, or death."*
> - Merry Wives of Windsor, V, 1.

So magical was the impression of odd numbers that Shakespeare to the better suggest the uncanny he puts into the mouth of a witch the two words "one" and "three" where four is meant.

> *"Thrice and once the hedge-pig whined."*
> - Macbeth, IV, 1.

In this he had classic authority for his guide. But there is another example of very considerable interest from our point of view. This is in the promise made by Cade to Dick, the butcher of Ashford. Butchers in the reign of Elizabeth were forbidden to sell during Lent unless by dispensation. Cade therefore makes a double promise, to lengthen Lent and also grant a very unusual permission to kill. The number in the promise could have obviously been one thing as another were it not for the deeper meaning associated with the odd number.

> *"Therefore, thus will I reward thee - the Lent shall be as long again as it is; and thou shalt have a license to kill for a hundred lacking ane."*
> - 2 Henry VI, IV, 3.

There are instances where the uses of the expression has indeed become so fixed a custom and habit in our conversation that the symbolism and strength of lore is no longer noted by us. Yet even here it is well worth the notice that Shakespeare prefers to employ an odd number where with equal ease he might have used something else. As,

> *"Threescore and ten I can remember well:*
> *Within the volume of which time I have seen*
> *Hours dreadful and things strange: but this sore night*
> *Hath trifled former knowings."*
> - Macbeth, II, 3.

Shakespeare has also reproduced an old charm or spell that may have been employed as an agency against attacks of nightmare. Here it is as will be seen the mention of a number is in both cases to an odd one.

> *"Saint Withold footed thrice the old wold;*
> *He met the night-mare, and her nine-fold;*
> *Bid her alight*
> *And troth her plight,*
> *And, aroint thee, witch, aroint thee!"*
> - King Lear, III, 4.

The Spiritual Side of Masonry

J. H. Morrow

One of the most beautiful of natural phenomena is the dew. We rise up early in the morning, throw open the casement, and there, spread out before us on earth's green carpet, lie myriads upon myriads of gems more brilliant than ever graced a queenly brow. It is as though God before rolling up the canopy of night had laid the stars for a moment upon the earth for man's nearer view.

As we gaze, entranced, the sun asserts his majesty, and along invisible paths the wealth of magic beauty vanishes in thin air. But each crystal drop has left refreshment in its wake. The tender blade of grass, the newborn leaf of the shrub, the unfolding petal of the blossom has each in turn gathered fresh life and renewed vigor.

And so, in a way, is spirituality. Heaven sent, it comes to earth to quicken men's souls into new life. It is all that the dew is to nature, but it is far more. It more closely resembles the gentle rain in the depth and permanence of its effect.

A dove brought a seed from the skies, and it said to the man, "The seed I bring is precious beyond all price. Its name is the Knowledge-of-God. I would fain plant it where it shall find constant nourishment, so that it may germinate and grow and bear fruit for the healing of the nations."

Reverently the man uncovered his head, and humbly bared his breast. "O gentle dove," he said, "vouchsafe that this seed may find lodgment in my poor heart." And the dove replied, "So let it be," and straightway it planted the seed in the human breast so freely offered.

And there flew to earth another dove, and the seed it brought-was called Faith, and this seed, too, found lodgment in the man's heart. And still another dove brought the seed of Hope, and another the seed of Charity, and a fourth the seed of Brotherly Love, and again a fifth the seed of Immortality; for these seeds, too, the man's breast gave welcoming place

The name of the man was Freemason. The life he lived, and the deeds he wrought, be they small or great, are known to all, but the vision of the doves and the planting of the seeds were for his eye alone.

Brethren, if I have indulged in metaphor and resorted to parable, it has been but to stimulate the imagination that you may the more easily rise with me to the plane upon which Masonry in its teachings and their fulfillment rests. The first seed implanted in the heart of the Freemason was the Knowledge-of-God. To put our trust in Him is the initial and the directing step in the journey of life. With Him as our guide, our mentor, we can press forward without doubt or fear. As Christian, Jew, Brahmin, or Mohammedan, each may call Him by a different name, but to one and all He is the Great Architect, the Supreme Ruler of the Universe, and as we learn to accept His guidance, He becomes better still the Heavenly Father, drawing us to Him with bonds of love. "We feel His presence, e'en unseen," and we walk by faith, and are sustained by hope in its whispered promise of eternal life. And so it is with the other seeds. In the exercise, for example, of charity through the promptings of brotherly love — charity which softens and modifies our judgments, makes us conscious of our own shortcomings, and renders us responsive to the appeals of those in distress — we become partakers of the Divine nature and thus children of God.

"To worship rightly is to love each other; Each smile a hymn, each kindly deed a prayer." "Each loving life a psalm of gratitude."

King Solomon's Temple is long crumbled into dust, but we as Masons are taught that we may rear another in its stead. The plan lies upon the trestle board of the Supreme Master. Happy is the man who builds according to that plan. For the temple site is the human heart, and the temple is known as character. Masonry is character-building, and whether we be Entered Apprentice, Fellowcraft, or Master Mason, our duties are clearly defined, and our accountability made clear.

Now, character is what we are, and must not be confounded with reputation, which is what men think of us. If character be sound, be good, be true, then reputation can safely be left to take care of itself. Men covet reputation, but reputation is only secure when it rests upon a moral foundation. Hypocrisy, deceit, false pretensions may achieve their ends for a while, but sooner or later the sham will be found out, and the structure so faultily built prove but a house of cards. Therefore, the question which concerns me as a Mason is not what do men think of me, but what do I think of myself?

In the light of Masonry I am able to judge myself. The plan lies before me. My obligations are emblazoned upon the walls of my remembrance. How have I hewn and laid the foundations of my character? How have I built the superstructure? Dare I apply to the walls the plumb and square and level of righteousness ? The heart of the man who received the seeds from the doves knew as the days and the years went by how well it had cherished the divine gifts. So, as I lay my head at night upon my pillow, and turn upon myself the eyes of introspection, I can search my soul.

Shall I be discouraged by the faults I find? Nay, not so. If I only realize that I have tried to build a temple acceptable to the Supreme Architect, I have not wholly failed. To be able to discover the fault shows that I have not lost sight of the plan, and am not deaf to the still small voice of conscience. And the wonderful thing in character-building is that so long as life lasts opportunity is given all to correct the faults. Fortunate, indeed, am I if the faults be those of days rather than of years. Yet it were better to begin all over again, though the structure eventually remain incomplete, than never to have made the attempt. But I must not put off the rebuilding to "a more convenient season," for "the night cometh when no man can work." Opportunity is mine, but it is limited. The sands remaining in my hourglass I cannot see.

Still, I must not despair. Hands of brotherly love are outstretched to help me.

Toil though we may, none toils alone— A brother's hands help lift the stone My arm is powerless to place; And love is beaming from his face.

Furthermore, we cannot contemplate the sublime truths of Masonry without receiving a reciprocal blessing. It is an immutable law that like begets like. Out of the abundance of the harvest is the promise of another garnering of like kind. And we sow without doubt, knowing that as we sow so shall we also reap. What is true of nature is true of spirituality. Of all the gifts of the inner life, the highest is that of love. Brotherly love unifies Masonry, and in its expression ennobles the lives of the brethren. It is this ennoblement, this enrichment so evident in innumerable instances, that draws men to our sanctuaries, humble and voluntary applicants for admission. They have discovered in the influences of Masonry a transforming power for good which they would fain enjoy.

Sculptured in profile on a New England mountain cliff is the noble face of a man. Tradition foretold that one day the counterpart would appear in human form. And the story runs that a lad was wont to visit the spot, watching in his boyish faith for the fulfillment of the promise. Alas, many passed, but never one who in lineament and expression reflected the heavenly beauty of the face of the granite hills. From boyhood the watcher grew to youth, and from youth to manhood, and still his dream remained unfulfilled. The tocsin of war sounded, and he hastened to the defense of his country's flag. Bravely, honorably, heroically he did his part, but often on picket duty in the gloomy watches of the night or amid the fitful sleep of the turf-pillowed bivouac, that radiant face of the distant mountain would reveal itself, and he would study it with the eyes of introspection. The war ended, and it was vouchsafed to him to return to his home. From force of habit he repaired to the mountain. There stood the face, as it had stood for ages untold, not an attribute impaired. Lost in reverie the soldier in his faded uniform became unconscious of surroundings, and unaware of the gathering of an awe-struck group. The tradition was at last come true; the counterpart in human form was there — but he did not know it.

Like begets like, beauty begets beauty, love begets love, holiness begets holiness, but the discovery is left to others.

Frequenting the almost inaccessible peak of a lofty mountain was a bird of snow-white plumage. Its name was Purity, and to him who should find one of its spotless feathers was the promise of eternal life. Many essayed to find a feather, but discouraged by the obstacles became disheartened and dropped back to the Valley of Ease — all save one. Undaunted, though bruised and bleeding, he pressed upward. Often he stumbled, sometimes he slipped backward, but only to regain lost ground and to keep on climbing. Would he ever reach the top ? His strength was giving out, when suddenly the shadow of the bird rested upon him. With one last effort he stretched forth his hand, but only to grasp thin air. He fell and died, and then, lo the miracle ! From the pitying breast of the hovering bird descended a feather, and rested on the palm of the nerveless hand. The gift of eternal life was won.

Brethren, the spiritual rewards of Masonry are not to be sought in the Valley of Ease. They may be summed up in one phrase — the satisfaction of feeling that we have endeavored to walk uprightly in every path of life, and to discharge our duties to God, to country, to home, to our fellow-men in conformity with the sublime teachings of the Order. The rest may be left to Him who noteth even the fall of a sparrow.

"Oh ! the cedars of Lebanon grow at our door, And the quarry is sunk at our gate; And the ships out of Ophir, with golden ore, For our summoning mandate wait; And the word of a Master Mason May the house of our soul create ! While the day hath light let the light be used, For no man shall the night control ! Or ever the silver cord be loosed, Or broken the golden bowl, May we build King Solomon's Temple In the true Masonic soul!"

And the meaning is this — that we do not have to go far afield to discharge our Masonic obligations, and to be spiritually quickened. In the pursuit of wealth men often travel to the uttermost parts of the world and endure danger and privation without end, alas, sometimes in vain, not realizing that mines of golden promise lie buried at the very doorsteps of the homes they have spurned. So the demands for the exercise of Masonic virtues lie close at hand. The stranger, hopeless, distressed, is knocking at our gate for admittance. The tearstained faces of the widow and the orphan are lifted in appeal to our windows. The brother, needy in a material or in a spiritual sense, is mutely stretching out his hand for help and sympathy along the pathway of our daily routine. Our homes are demanding of us the highest expressions of love. Our city and our country are expecting us to exemplify civic righteousness. And the voice of God is ever ringing in our ears, "Inasmuch as ye have done it unto one of the least of these, my brethren, ye have done it unto Me."

It is a misnomer to speak of the spiritual side of Masonry. If there be another side it is foreign to our Order, and I know it not. Spirituality is the life of Masonry. Blest is he who is privileged to partake of it, and to help rebuild the Temple of King Solomon.

The Eleusinian Mysteries and Rites
Dudley Wright

Many writers, and especially those of the Craft, have called attention to the resemblances between the rites of the Ancient Mysteries and those of Freemasonry. Indeed, those resemblances have given rise to much speculation, and it has been suggested by more than one writer that such resemblances are more than accidental Some of us have long been convinced that Freemasonry, if we may not say that it was historically descended from the instituted Mysteries of antiquity, it at least perpetuates their ministry among us.

The Eleusinian Mysteries - those rites of ancient Greece and afterwards of Rome, of which there is historical evidence dating back to the seventh century before the Christian era bear very striking resemblance, in many points, to the rituals of both Operative and Speculative Freemasonry - As to their origin, beyond the legendary account put forth, there is no reliable trace. Like most great human institutions they grew out of a real human need, to which they ministered, else they could not have held sway for so many ages.

In the opinion of not a few writers an Egyptian source is attributed to them, but of this there is no positive proof, though we may infer as much, remembering the influence of Egypt upon Greece. There is a legend that St. John the Evangelist a character honored and revered by Freemasons was an initiate of these mysteries. Certainly, more than one of the early Fathers of the Christian Church boasted of his initiation into these Rites. Even St. Paul was influenced by them, to the extent, at least, of using some of their imagery, and even some of their technical terms, in his Epistles.

The series of articles, to which I have the honor thus to call attention, is one of the first attempts so far made to give a detailed exposition of the ceremonial of the Mysteries of Greece in English. As such they have an interest to Masons, but also to students of antiquity in general, and if the field were familiar, as it is not, these articles would be worthy of special interest for the new materials brought forward- Brother Wright, I need hardly say, is a careful, painstaking, and thorough student, as readers can testify, and among his many services to the Craft this study will not be reckoned the least.

Such a writer needs no introduction, but I have much pleasure in emphasizing the importance of these researches in ancient lore, because they make a real contribution to our knowledge. -Joseph Fort Newton.

THE ELEUSINIAN LEGEND

The legend which formed the basis of the Mysteries of Eleusis, presence at and participation in which, demanded an elaborate form or ceremony of initiation, was as follows:

Persephone (sometimes described as Proserpine and as Cora or Kore) when gathering flowers was abducted by Pluto, the god of Hades, and carried off by him to his gloomy abode; Zeus, the brother of Pluto and the father of Persephone, giving his consent. Demeter (or Ceres), her mother, arrived too late to assist her child or even to catch a glimpse of her seducer, and neither god nor man was able, or willing, to enlighten her as to the whereabouts of Persephone or who had carried her away. For nine nights and days she wandered, torch in hand, in quest of her child. Eventually, however, she heard from Helios (the sun) the name of the seducer and his accomplice. Incensed at Zeus she left Olympos and the gods and came down to scour the earth disguised as an old woman.

In the course of her wanderings she arrived at Eleusis where she was honorably entertained by Keleos, the ruler of the country, with whom and his wife, Metanira, she consented to remain in order to watch over the education of Demophon, who had just been born to the aged king, and whom she undertook to make immortal.

Long was thy anxious search For lovely Proserpine, nor didst thou break Thy mournful fast, till the far-fam'd Eleusis Received thee wandering.

Unknown to the parents Demeter used to anoint Demophon by day with ambrosia and hide him by night in the fire like a firebrand. Detected one night by Metanira she was compelled to reveal herself as Demeter, the goddess. Whereupon she directed the Eleusinians to erect a temple as a peace offering and, this being done, she promised to initiate them into the form of worship which would obtain for them her goodwill and favor. "It is I, Demeter, full of glory, who lightens and gladdens the hearts of gods and men. Hasten ye, my people, to raise hard by the citadel, below the ramparts, a fane, and on the eminence of the hill, an altar, above the wall of Callichorum. I will instruct you in the rites which shall be observed and which are pleasing to me."

The temple was erected but Demeter was still vowing vengeance against gods and men and because of the continued loss of her daughter she rendered the earth sterile during a whole year.

What ails her that she comes not home? Demeter seeks her far and wide; And gloomy-browed doth ceaseless roam From many a morn till eventide. "My life, immortal though it be, Is naught!" she cries, "for want of thee, Persephone Persephone !"

The oxen drew the plough but in vain was the seed sown in the prepared ground. Mankind was threatened with utter annihilation and all the gods were deprived of sacrifices and offerings. Zeus endeavoured to appease the anger of the gods but in vain. Finally he summoned Hermes to go to Pluto to order him to restore Persephone to her mother. Pluto yielded but before Persephone left she took from the hand of Pluto four pomegranate pips which he offered her as sustenance on her journey. Persephone, returning from the land of shadows, found her mother in the temple at Eleusis which had recently been erected. Her first question was whether her daughter had eaten anything in the land of her imprisonment, because her unconditional return to earth and Olympos depended upon that. Persephone informed her mother that all she had eaten was the pomegranate pips in consequence of which Pluto demanded that Persephone should sojourn with him for four months during each year, or one month for each pip taken. Demeter had no option but to consent to this arrangement, which meant that she would enjoy the company of Persephone for eight months in every year and that the remaining four would be spent by Persephone with Pluto. Demeter caused to awaken anew "the fruits of the fertile plains" and the whole earth was reclothed with leaves and flowers. Demeter called together the princes of Eleusis Triptolemus, Diocles, Eumolpus, Polyxenos, and Keleos and initiated them "into the sacred rites most venerable into which no one is allowed to make enquiries or to divulge; a solemn warning from the gods seals our mouths."

Although secrecy on the subject of the nature of the stately Mysteries is strictly enjoined, the writer of the Homeric Hymn to Demeter makes no secret of the happiness which comes to all who become initiates: "Happy is he who has been received, unfortunate he who has never received the initiation nor taken part in the sacred ordinances, and who cannot, alas! be destined to the same lot reserved for the faithful in the darkling abode."

The version of the legend given by Minucius Felix is as follows:

"Proserpine, the daughter of Ceres by Jupiter, as she was gathering tender flowers in the new spring, was ravished from her delightful abodes by Pluto; and, being carried from thence through thick woods and over a length of sea, was brought by Pluto into a cavern, the residence of departed spirits, over whom she afterwards ruled with absolute sway. But Ceres, upon discovering the loss of her daughter, with lighted torches and begirt with a serpent, wandered over the whole earth for the purpose of finding her till she came to Eleusis; there she found her daughter and discovered to the Eleusinians the plantation of corn."

In the Homeric Hymn to Demeter, Persephone gives her own version of the incident as follows:

"We were all playing in the lovely meadows, Leucippe, and Phaino, and Electra, and Ianthe, and Melite, and Iache, and Rhodeia, and Callinhoe, and Melobosis, and Ianeira, and Acaste, and Admete, and Rhodope, and Plouto, and winsome Calypso, and Styx, and Urania, and beautiful Galaxame. We were playing there and plucking beautiful blossoms with our hands; crocuses mingled, and iris, and hyacinth, and roses, and lilies, a marvel to behold, and narcissus, that the wide earth bare, a wile for my undoing. Gladly was I gathering them when the earth gaped beneath and therefrom leaped the mighty prince, the host of many guests, and he bare me against my will, despite my grief, beneath the earth, in his golden chariot; and shrilly did I cry."

On the submission of Eleusis to Athens, the Mysteries became an integral part of the Athenian religion, so that the Eleusinian Mysteries became a Panhellenic institution, and later, under the Romans, a universal worship, but the secret rites of initiation were well kept throughout their history.

The earliest mention of the Temple of Demeter at Eleusis occurs in the Homeric Hymn to Demeter, which has already been mentioned. This was not written by Homer but by some poet versed in Homeric lore and its probable date is about 600 B. C. It was discovered a little over a hundred years ago in an old monastery library at Moscow, and now reposes in a museum at Leyden.

Eleusis was one of the twelve originally independent cities of Attica, which Theseus is said to have united into a single state. Leusina now occupies the site and has thus preserved the name of the ancient city. Theseus is portrayed by Virgil as suffering eternal punishment in Hades but Proclus writes concerning him as follows:

Theseus and Pirithous are fabled to have ravished Helen and to have descended to the infernal regions: i. e., they were lovers of intelligible and visible beauty. Afterwards Theseus was liberated by Pericles from Hades, but Pirithous remained there because he could not sustain the arduous attitude of divine contemplation.

Dr. Warburton, in his Divine Legation of Moses, gives, as his opinion, that Theseus was a living character who once forced his way into the Eleusinian Mysteries, for which crime he was imprisoned on earth and afterwards damned in the infernal regions.

The Eleusinian Mysteries seem to have constituted the most vital portion of the Attic religion and always to have retained something of awe and solemnity. They were not known outside Attica until the time of the Median wars, when they spread to the Greek colonies in Asia as part of the constitution of the daughter states, where the cult seems to have exercised a considerable influence both on the populace and on the philosophers. Outside Eleusis the Mysteries were not celebrated so frequently nor on so magnificent a scale. At Celeas, where they were celebrated every third year, a hierophant, who was not bound by the law of celibacy, as at Eleusis, was elected by the people for each celebration. Pausanias is the authority for a statement by the Phliasians that they imitated the Eleusinian Mysteries. They, however, maintained that their rendering was instituted by Dysaules, brother of Celeus, who went to their country after he had been expelled from Eleusis by Ion, son of Xuthus, at the time when Ion was chosen commander-in-chief of the Athenians in the war against Eleusis. Pausanias disputed that any Eleusinian was defeated in battle and forced into exile, maintaining that peace was concluded between the Athenians and the Eleusinians before the war was fought out, even Eumolpus himself being permitted to remain in Eleusis. Pausanias, also, while admitting that Dysaules might have gone to Phlius for some cause other than that admitted by the Phliasians, questioned whether Dysaules was related to Celeus, or, indeed, to any illustrious Eleusinian family. The name of Dysaules does not occur in the Homeric Hymn to Demeter, where are enumerated all who were taught the ritual of the Mysteries by the goddess, though that of Celeus is mentioned:

She showed to Triptolemus and Dioeles, smiter of horses, And mighty Eumolpus and Celeus, leader of people, The way of performing the sacred rites and explained to all of them the orgies.

Nevertheless, according to the Phliasians, it was Dysaules who instituted the Mysteries among them.

The Pheneatians also had a sanctuary dedicated to Demeter, which they called Eleusinian and in which they celebrated the Mysteries in honor of the goddess. They had a legend that Demeter went thither in her wanderings and that out of gratitude to the Pheneatians for the hospitality they showed her, she gave them all the different kinds of pulse, except beans. Two Pheneatians Trisaules and Damithales built a temple to Demeter Thesuria, the goddess of laws, under Mount Cyllene, where were instituted the Mysteries in her honor, which were celebrated until a late period and which were said to be introduced there by Naus, a grandson of Eumolpus.

"Much that is excellent and divine," wrote Cicero, "does Athens seem to me to have produced and added to our life, but nothing better than those Mysteries by which we are formed and moulded from a rude and savage state of humanity; and, indeed, in the Mysteries we perceive the real principles of life, and learn not only to live happily, but to die with a fairer hope." Every manner of writer religious poet, worldly poet, sceptical philosopher, orator all are of one mind about this, far the greatest of all the religious festivals of Greece.

The Eleusinian Mysteries, observed by nearly all Greeks, but particularly by the Athenians, were celebrated yearly at Eleusis, though in the earlier annals of their history, they were celebrated once in every three years only, and once in every four years by the Celeans, Cretans, Parrhasians, Pheneteans, Phliasians, and Spartans. It was the most celebrated of all the religious ceremonies of Greece at any period of the country's history and was regarded as of such importance that the Festival is referred to frequently simply as "The Mysteries."

The rites were guarded most jealously and carefully concealed from the unnitiated. If any person divulged any part of them he was regarded as having offended against the divine law and by the act he rendered himself liable to divine vengeance. It was accounted unsafe to abide in the same house with him and as soon as his offence was made public he was apprehended. Similarly, drastic punishment was meted out to any person not initiated into the mysteries who chanced to be present at their celebration, even through ignorance or genuine error.

PART II THE ELEUSINIAN MYSTERTIES

The Mysteries were divided into two parts-the Lesser Mysteries and the Greater Mysteries. The lesser Mysteries were said to have been instituted when Hercules, Castor, and Pollux expressed a desire to be initiated, they happening to be in Athens at the time of the celebration of the Mysteries by the Athenians in accordance with the ordinance of Demeter. Not being Athenians they were ineligible for the honor of initiation, but the difficulty was overcome by Eumolpus, who was desirous of including in the ranks of the initited a man of such power and eminence as Hercules, foreigner though he might be. The three were first made citizens, and then, as a preliminary to the initiation ceremony as prescribed by the goddess, Eumolpus instituted the Lesser Mysteries, which then and afterwards became a ceremony preliminary to the Greater Mysteries, as they then became known, for candidates of alien birth. In later times, this lesser festival, celebrated in the month of Anthesterion, at the beginning of spring, at Agra, became a general preparation for the Greater Festival and no persons were initiated into the Greater Mysteries until they had first been initiated into the Lesser.

The ceremonies of the Lesser Mysteries were entirely different from those of the Greater Mysteries. The Lesser Mysteries represented the return of Persephone to earth which, of course, took place at Eleusis, and the Greater Mysteries represented her descent to the infernal regions. The Lesser Mysteries honored the daughter more than the mother, who was the principal figure in the Greater Mysteries. In the Lesser Mysteries, Persephone was known as Pherrephatta, and in the Greater Mysteries she was given the name of Kore. Everything was in fact a mystery and nothing was called by its right name.

Lenormant says that it is certain that the initiated of the Lesser Mysteries carried away from Agra a certain store of religious knowledge which enabled them to understand the symbols and representations which afterwards were displayed before their eyes at the Greater Mysteries at Eleusis.

The object of the Lesser Mysteries was to signify occultly the condition of the impure soul invested with a terrene body and merged in a material nature. The Greater Mysteries taught that he, who, in the present life, is in subjection to his irrational part, is truly in Hades. If Hades, then, is the region of punishment and misery, the purified soul must reside in the region of bliss, theoretically in the present life and according to a deific energy in the next. They intimated by gorgeous mystic visions the felicity of the soul, both here and hereafter, when purified from the defilements of a material nature and consequently elevated to the realities of intellectual vision.

No one was permitted to attend the Mysteries who had incurred the capital punishment for treason or conspiracy, but all other exiles were permitted to be present and were not molested in any way during the whole period of the Festival. No one could be arrested for debt during the holding of the Festival.

Scarcely anything is known of the program observed during the course of the Lesser Mysteries. They were celebrated on the 19th to 21st of the month Anthesterion and, like the Greater Mysteries, were preceded and followed by a truce on the part of all engaged in warfare. The same officials presided at both celebrations. The Lesser Mysteries opened with a sacrifice to Demeter and Persephone, a portion of the victims offered being reserved for the members of the sacred families of Eumolpus and Keryce. The main object of the Lesser Mysteries was to put the candidates for initiation in a condition of ritual purification and, according to Clement of Alexandria, they included certain instructions and preparations for the Greater Mysteries. Like the Eleusinian Mysteries, properly so- called, they included dramatic representations of the rape of Persephone and the wanderings of Demeter, in addition, according to Stephen Byzantium, to certain Dionysian representations.

Two months before the full moon of the month of Boedromion, sphondophoroi or heralds selected from the priestly families of the Eumolpides and Keryces went forth to announce the forthcoming celebration of the Greater Mysteries and to claim an armistice on the part of all who might be waging war. The truce commenced on the 15th of the month preceding the celebration of the Mysteries and lasted until the tenth day of the month following the celebration. In order to be valid the truce had to be proclaimed in and accepted by each Hellenic city.

All arrangements for the proper celebration of the Mysteries, both Lesser and Greater, were in the hands of the families of Eumolpides and Keryces. These were ancient Eleusinian families, whose origin was traced back to the time when Eleusis was independent of Athens, and the former family survived as a priestly caste down to the latest period of Athenian history. Its members possessed the hereditary and sole right to the secrets of the Mysteries. Hence the recognition by the State to their exclusive right and privilege to direct the initiations and to provide each a half of the religious staff of the temple. Pausanias relates that following a war between the Eleusinians and the Athenians when Erectheus, King of Athens, conquered Immaradus, son of Eumolpus, the subdued Eleusinians, in making their submission, stipulated that they should remain custodians of the Mysteries, but in all other respects were to be subject to the Athenians. This tradition is disputed by more modern writers, but it was accepted by the Athenians and acted upon generally, and the right of the two families solely to prepare candidates for initiation was recognized by a decree of the fifth century B. C., the privilege being confirmed afterwards at a convention between the representatives of Eleusis and Athens. The Eumolpides were the descendants of a mythical ancestor, Eumolpus, son of Neptune, who is first mentioned in the time of Pisastrus. On the death of Eumolpus, Ceryx, the younger of the sons was left. But the Keryces claimed that Ceryx was a son of Hermes by Aglamus, daughter of Cecrops, and that he was not a son of Eumolpus.

The members of the family of Eumolpides had the first claim upon the flesh of the sacrificed animals; but they were permitted to give a portion to any one else as a reward or recompense for services rendered. But when a sacrifice was offered to any of the infernal divinities the whole of it had to be consumed by the fire; nothing must be left. All religious problems relating to the Mysteries which could not be solved by the known laws were addressed to the Eumolpides, whose decision was final.

The meaning of the name "Eumolpus" is "a good singer," and great importance was attached to the quality of the voice in the selection of the hierophant, the chief officiant at the celebration of the Mysteries and at the ceremony of initiation, and who was selected from the family of the Eumolpides. It was essential that the formulae disclosed to the initiates at Eleusis should be pronounced with the proper intonation, for otherwise the words would have no efficacy. Correct intonation was of far greater importance than syllabic pronunciation. An explanation of this is given by Maspero who says:

The human voice is pre-eminently a magical instrument, without which none of the highest operations of art can be successful: each of its utterances is carried into the region of the invisible and there released forces of which the general run of people have no idea, either as to their existence or their manifold action. Without doubt, the real value of an evocation lies in its text, or the sequence of the words of which it is composed and the tone in which it is enunciated. In order to be efficacious, the conjuration should be accompanied by chanting, either an incantation or a song. In order to produce the desired effect the sacramental melody must be chanted without the variation of a single modulation: one false note, one mistake in the measure, the introversion of any two of the sounds of which it is composed, and the intended effect is annulled. This is the reason why all who recite a prayer or formula intended to force the gods to perform certain acts must be of true voice. The result of their effort, whether successful or unsuccessful, will depend upon the exactness of their voice. It was the voice, therefore, which played the most important part in the oblation, in the prayer of definite request, and in the evocation- in a word, in every instance where man sought to seize hold of the god. Apart from a true voice the words were merely dead sounds.

The Hierophant was a revealer of holy things. He was a citizen of Athens, a man of mature age, and held his office for life, devoting himself wholly to the service of the temple and living a chaste life, to which end it was usual for him to anoint himself with the juice of hemlock, which, by its extreme coldness, was said to extinguish in a great measure the natural heat. In the opinion of some writers celibacy was an indispensable condition of the highest branch of the priesthood, but, according to inscriptions which have been discovered, some, at any rate, of the hierophants were married, so that, in all probability, the rule was that during the celebration of the Mysteries and, probably, for a certain time before and after, it was incumbent on the hierophant to abstain from all sexual intercourse. Foucart is of opinion that celibacy was demanded only during the celebration of the Mysteries, although Pausanias states definitely otherwise. In support of Foucart it may be stated that among the inscriptions discovered at Eleusis there is one dedicating a statue to a hierophant by his wife. It was essential that the hierophant should be a man of commanding presence and lead a simple life. On being raised to the dignity he received a kind of consecration at a special ceremony, at which only those of his own rank were permitted to be present, when he was entrusted with certain secrets pertaining to his high office. Prior to this ceremony he went through a special purifactory rite, immersing himself in the sea, an act to which the Greeks attributed great virtue. He had to be exemplary in his moral conduct and was regarded by the people as being peculiarly holy. The qualifications of a hierophant were so high that the office could not be regarded as hereditary, for it would have been an exception to find both father and son in possession of the many various and high qualifications regarded as essential to the holding of the office. The robe of the hierophant was a long purple garment; his hair, crowned with a wreath of myrtle, flowed in long locks over his shoulders, and a diadem ornamented his forehead. At the celebration of the Mysteries he was held to represent the Creator of the world. He alone was permitted to penetrate into the innermost shrine in the Hall of the Mysteries the holy of holies, as it were and then only once during the celebration of the Mysteries, when, at the most solemn moment of the whole mystic celebration, his form appeared suddenly to be transfigured with light before the rapt gaze of the initiated. He alone was permitted to reveal to the fully initiated the mystic objects, the sight of which marked the completion of their admission into the community. He had the power of refusing admission to those applicants whom he deemed unfit to be entrusted with the secrets. He was not inactive during the intervals between the celebration of the Mysteries. It was his duty to superintend the instruction of the candidates for initiation who, for that purpose, were divided into groups and instructed by officials known as mystagogues. The personal name of the hierophant was never mentioned: it was supposed to be unknown, "wafted away into the sea by the mystic law," and he was known only by the title of the office which he bore. Lucian refers to this in one passage in Lexiphanes:

The first I met were a torch-bearer, a hierophant, and others of the initiated, haling Dinias before the judge, and protesting that he had called them by their names, though he well knew that, from the time of their sanctification, they were nameless, and no more to be named but by hallowed names.

In the Imperial inscriptions we find the titles substituted for the proper names. The hierophant was compelled to avoid contact with the dead, in the same manner as the Cohanim of the Jewish faith, and with certain animals reputed to be unclean. Contact with any person from whom blood was issuing also caused impurity. He was assisted by a female hierophant, or hierophantide an attendant upon the goddess Demeter and her daughter, Persephone. She also was selected from the family of the Eumolpides and was chosen for life She was permitted to marry and several inscriptions mention the names of children of hierophantides. On her initiation into this high degree she was brought forward naked to the side of a sacred font, in which her right hand was placed, the priest declaring her to be true and holy and dedicated to the service of the temple. The special duty of the female hierophant was to superintend the initiation of female aspirants, but she was present throughout the ceremony and played some part in the initiation of the male candidates. An inscription on the tomb of one hierophantide mentions to her glory that she had set the myrtle crown, the seal of mystic communion, on the heads of the illustrious initiates, Marcus Aurelius and his son, Commodus. Another gloried in the fact that she had initiated the emperor Hadrian.

Next in rank to the hierophant and hierophantide came the male and female Dadouchos, who were taken from the family of the Keryces. They were the torchbearers and their duty consisted mainly in carrying the torches at the Sacred Festival. They also wore purple robes, myrtle crowns, and diadems. They were appointed for life and were permitted to marry. The male Dadouchos, particularly, was associated with the hierophant in certain solemn and public functions, such as the opening address to the candidates for initiation and in the public prayers for the welfare of the state. The office was frequently handed down from father to son. Until the first century, B. C., the Dadouchos was never addressed by his own personal name, but always by the title of his office.

The Hierocceryx, or messenger of holy tidings, was the representative of Hermes, or Mercury, who, as the messenger of the gods, was indispensable as mediator whenever men wished to approach the Immortals. He also wore a purple-colored robe and a myrtle crown. He was chosen for life from the family of the Keryces. He made the necessary proclamations to the candidates for initiation into the various degrees and, in particular, enjoined them to preserve silence. It was necessary for him to have passed through all the various degrees as his duties necessitated his presence throughout the ceremonial.

The Phaidantes had the custody of the sacred statues and the sacred vessels, which they had to maintain in good repair. They were selected from one or other of the two sacerdotal families.

Among the other officials were: the Liknophori, who carried the mystic fan; the Hydranoi, who purified the candidates for initiation by sprinkling them with holy water at the commencement of the festival; the Spondophoroi, who proclaimed the sacred truce, which was to permit of the peaceful celebration of the Mysteries; the Pyrphoroi, who brought and maintained the fire for the sacrifices; the Hieraules, who played the flute during the time the sacrifices were being offered they were the leaders of the sacred music, who had under their charge the hynmodoi, the hymnetriai; the neokoroi, who maintained the temples and the altars; the panageis, who formed a class between the ministers and the initiated. Then there were the "initiates of the altar," who performed expiatory rites in the name and in the place of all the initiated. There were also many other minor officials, known by the general name of Melissae, i.e., bees, perhaps so-called because bees, being makers of honey, were sacred to Demeter. All these officials had to be of unblemished reputation and wore myrtle crowns while engaged in the service of the temple.

The officials, whose duty it was to take care that the ritual was punctiliously followed in every detail, included nine Archons, who were chosen every year to manage the affairs of Greece. The first of these was always the King, or Archon Basileus, whose duty at the celebration of the Mysteries it was to offer prayers and sacrifices, to see that no indecency or irregularity was committed during the Festival and at the conclusion to pass judgment on all offenders. There were also four Epimeletae, or curators, elected by the people, one being appointed from the Eumolpides, another from the Keryces, and the remaining two from the rank and file of the citizens; and ten Hieropoioi, whose duty it was to offer sacrifices.

The sacred symbols used in the ceremonies were enclosed in a special chamber in the Telestrion or Hall of Initiation, known as the Anactoron, into which the hierophant alone had the right to penetrate. During the celebration of the Mysteries they were carried to Athens veiled and hidden from the gaze of the profane, whence they were taken back to Eleusis. It was permitted only to the initiated to look upon these "hiera," as they were called. These sacred objects were in the charge of the Eumolpides family.

Written descriptions, however graphic or eloquent, convey but a faint impression of the wonderful scenes that were enacted; Aristides says that what was seen rivalled anything that was heard. For nine centuries that period of time being divided almost equally between the pre-Christian and Christian eras they were the Palladium of Greek Paganism. In the latter part of their history, when the restriction, as to admission began to be relaxed, and in proportion to that relaxation, their essential religious character disappeared and they became a mere ceremony, their splendor being their principal attraction, until finally they degenerated into a mere superstition. Julian strived in vain to infuse new life into the vanishing cult, but it was too late the Eleusinian Mysteries were dead.

The Festival of the Greater Mysteries, and this was, of course, by far the more important, began on the 15th of the month Boedromion, corresponding roughly with the month of September, and lasted until the 23rd of the same month. During that time it was unlawful to arrest any man present, or present any petition except for offenses committed at the Festival, heavy penalties being inflicted for breaches of this law, the penalties fixed being a fine of not less than a thousand drachmas, and some assert that transgressors were even put to death.

The following was the program of the Festival:

First Day. The first day was known as the "Gathering" or the "Assembly," when all who had passed through the Lesser Mysteries assembled to assist in the celebration of the greater Mysteries. On this day the Archon Basileus presided over all the cults of the city and assembled the people at a place known as the Poikile Stoa. After the

Archon Basileus, with four assistants, had offered up sacrifices and prayers for the welfare of Greece, the following proclamation was made by the Archon Basileus, wearing his robe of office:

Come whoever is clean of all pollution and whose soul has not consciousness of sin. Come, whosoever hath lived a life of righteousness and justice. Come all ye who are pure of heart and of hand, and whose speech can be understood. Whosoever hath not clean hands, a pure soul, and an intelligible voice, must not assist at the Mysteries.

The people were then commanded by the hierophant to wash their hands in consecrated water and the impious were threatened with the punishment set forth in the law if they were discovered, but especially, and this in any case, with the implacable anger of the gods. The Hierocceryx then impressed upon all the duty of observing the most rigid secrecy with respect to all that they might witness and bade all be silent throughout the ceremonies and not utter even an exclamation. The candidates for initiation assembled outside the temple, each under the guidance and direction of a mystagogue, who repeated these instructions to the candidates. Once within the sacred enclosure all the initiated were subject to a purification by fire ceremonial. All wore regalia special to the occasion; this is evident from the wording of inscriptions which have been discovered, but particulars of this regalia are wanting. We know that extravagant and costly dresses were regarded by Demeter with disfavor and that it was forbidden to wear such in the temple. Jewelry, gold ornaments, purple colored belts and embroideries were also barred, as were robes and cloths of mixed colors. The hair of women had to fall down loose upon the shoulders and must not be in plaits or coiled upon the head. No woman was permitted to use cosmetics.

Second Day. The second day was known as Halade Mystae, or "To the sea, ye mystae" from the command which greeted all the initiated to go and purify themselves by washing in the sea, or in the salt water of the two lakes, called Rheiti, on what was known as "The Sacred Way." A procession was formed in which all joined and made their way to the sea or the lakes where they bathed and purified themselves. This general purification was akin to that practised to this day by the Jews at the beginning of the Jewish year. The day was consecrated to Saturn, into whose province the soul is said to fall in the course of its descent from the tropic of Cancer. Capella compares Saturn to a river, voluminous, sluggish, and cold. The planet signifies pure intellect and Pythagoras symbolically called the sea a tear of Saturn. The bathing was preceded by a confession and the manner in which the bathing was carried out and the number of immersions varied with the degree of guilt which each confessed. According to Suidas, those who had to purify themselves from murder plunged into salt water on two separate occasions, immersing themselves seven times on each occasion On returning from the bath all were regarded as "new creatures," the bath being regarded as a laver of regeneration, and the initiated were clothed in a plain fawn skin or a sheep skin. The purification, however, was not regarded as complete until the following day when there was added the sprinkling of the blood of a pig sacrificed. Each had carried to the river or lake a little pig which was also purified by bathing and on the next day this pig was sacrificed. On the Eleusinian coinage, the pig, standing on a torch placed horizontally, appears as the sign and symbol of the Mysteries. On this day also some of the initiated submitted to a special purification near the altar of Zeus Mellichios on the Sacred Way. For each person whom it was desired to purify, an ox was sacrificed to Zeus Mellichios, the infernal Zeus, and the skin of the animal was laid on the ground by the Dadouchos, and the one who was the object of the illustration remained there squatting on the left foot.

Third Day. On the third day pleasures of every description, even the most innocent, were strictly forbidden, and every one fasted till nightfall, when they partook of seed cakes, parched corn, salt, pomegranates, and sacred wine mixed with milk and honey. The Archon Basileus, assisted again by the four Epimeletae, celebrated in the presence of representatives from the allied cities, the great sacrifice of the Soteria for the well-being of the State, the Athenian citizens, and their wives and children. This ceremony took place in the Eleusinion at the foot of the Acropolis. The day was known as the Day of Mourning and was supposed to commemorate Demeter's grief at the loss of Persephone. The sacrifices offered consisted chiefly of a mullet and of barley out of Rharium, a field of Eleusis. The oblations were accounted so sacred that the priests themselves were not permitted, as was usual in other offerings, to partake of them. At the conclusion of the general ceremony each one individually sacrificed the little pig purified in the sea the night before.

Fourth Day. The principal event of the fourth day was a solemn procession when the holy basket of Ceres (Demeter) was carried in a consecrated cart, the crowds of people shouting as it went along, "Hail, Ceres!" The rear end of the procession was composed of women carrying baskets containing sesamin, carded wool, grains of salt, serpents, pomegranates reeds, ivy boughs, and cakes known as poppies.

Fifth Day. The fifth day was known as the Day of Torches from the fact that at nightfall all the initiated walked in pairs round the temple of Demeter at Eleusis, the Dadouchos himself leading the procession. The torches were waved about and changed from hand to hand to represent the wanderings of the goddess in search of her daughter when she was conducted by the light of a torch kindled in the flames of Etna.

Sixth Day. Iacchos was the name given to the sixth day of the Festival. The "fair young god" Iacchos, or Dionysos, or Sacchus, was the son of Jupiter and Ceres, and accompanied the goddess in her search for Persephone. He also carried a torch, hence his statue has always a torch in the hand. This statue, together with other sacred objects, were taken from the Iacchion, the sanctuary of Iacchos in Athens, mounted on a heavy rustic four- wheeled chariot drawn by bulls, and, accompanied by the Iacchogogue and other magistrates nominated for the occasion, conveyed from the Caramicus to Eleusis by the Sacred Way in solemn procession. The statue, as well as the people accompanying it, was crowned with myrtle, the people dancing all the way along the route, beating brass kettles and playing instruments of various kinds and singing sacred songs. Halts were made during the procession at various shrines, particularly at a fig-tree which was regarded as sacred, also upon a bridge built over the river Cephissus where the bystanders made themselves merry at the expense of the pilgrims. At each of the shrines sacrifices and libations were offered, hymns sung, and sacred dances performed. Having passed the bridge the people entered Eleusis by what was known as the Mystical Entrance. Midnight had set in before Eleusis was reached so that a great part of the journey had to be accomplished by the light of the torches carried by each of the pilgrims and the nocturnal journey was spoken of as the "night of torches" by many ancient authors. The pitch and resin of which the torches were composed were substances supposed to have the virtue of warding off evil spirits. The barren mountains of the Pass of Daphni and the surface of the sea resounded with the chant: "Iacchos, O Iacchos!" At one of the halts, the Croconians, descendants of the hero Crocon, who had formerly reigned over the Thriasian Plain, fastened a saffron band on the right arm and left foot of each one in the procession. Iacchos was always regarded as a child of Demeter, inasmuch as the vine grows out of the earth. Various symbols were carried by the people, who numbered sometimes as many as thirty and forty thousand. These symbols consisted of winnowing fans the "mystic fan of Iacchos"; plaited reeds and baskets, both relating to the worship of the goddess and her son. The distance covered by the procession was 22 kilometres, but Lyourgus ordered that if any woman should ride in a chariot to Eleusis she should be mulcted in a fine of 8,000 drachmas. This was to prevent the richer women from distinguishing themselves from their poorer sisters. Strange to relate, the wife of Lyourgus was the first to break this law and Lyourgus himself had to pay the fine which he had ordained. He not only paid the penalty but gave a talent to the informer. Immediately upon the deposit of the sacred objects in the Eleusinion at the foot of the Acropolis, one of the Eleusinion priests solemnly announced their arrival to the priestess of the tutelary goddess of Athens Pallas Athene. Plutarch, in commenting upon lucky and unlucky days, says that he is aware that unlucky things happen sometimes on lucky days, for the Athenians had to receive a Macedonian garrison "even on the 20th of Boedromion, the day on which they lead forth the mystic Iacchos."

Seventh Day. On the seventh day the statue was carried back to Athens. The return journey was also a solemn procession and attended with numerous ceremonies. Halts were again made at several places, like the "stations" of Roman Catholic pilgrimage, when the inhabitants also fell into line with the procession. For those who remained behind at Eleusis the time was devoted to sports, the victors in which were rewarded with a measure of barley, it being a tradition that grain was first sown in Eleusis. It was also regarded as a day of preparation for the initiation ceremony of the following night. The return journey was conducted with the same splendor as the outward journey. It comprised comic incidents, the same as on the previous day. Those who awaited the procession at the bridge over the Athenian river Cephisson exchanged all kinds of chaff and buffoonery with those who were in the procession, indulging in what was termed "bridge fooling." These jests, it is said, were to recall the tactful measure employed by a maid-servant named Iambe, to rouse Demeter from her prolonged mourning. During the Peliponnesian war the Athenians were unable to obtain an armistice from the Lacedaemonians who held Decelea and it became necessary to send the statue of Iacchos and the processionists to Eleusis by sea. Plutarch says: "Under these conditions it was necessary to omit the sacrifices usually offered all along the road during the passing of Iacchos."

Eighth Day. The eighth day was called Epidaurion because it happened once that Aesculapius, coming from Epidaurius to Athens, desired to be initiated and had the Lesser Mysteries repeated for that purpose. It therefore became customary to celebrate the Lesser Mysteries a second time upon this day and to admit to initiation any such approved candidates who had not already enjoyed the privilege. There was also another reason for the repetition of the initiatory rites then. The eighth day was regarded as symbolical of the soul falling into the lunar orbit and the repeated initiation, the second celebration of that sacred rite, was symbolical of the soul bidding adieu to everything of a celestial nature, sinking into a perfect oblivion of her divine origin and pristine felicity, and rushing profoundly into the region of dissimilitude, ignorance, and error. The day opened with a solemn sacrifice offered to Demeter and Persephone, which took place within the peribolus. The utmost precision had to be observed in offering this sacrifice as regarding the age, color, and sex of the victim; the chants, perfumes, and libations. The acceptance or rejection of a sacrifice was indicated by the movements of the animal as it approached the altar, the vivacity of the flame, the direction of the smoke, etc. If these signs were not favorable in the case of the first victim offered other animals must be slain until one presented itself in which all the signs were favorable. The flesh of the animal offered was not allowed to be taken outside the sacred precincts but had to be consumed within the building.

The following is said to have been an Invocation used during the celebration of the Mysteries:

Daughter of Jove, Persephone divine, Come, blessed queen, and to these rites incline; Only-begotten, Pluto's honored wife, O venerable goddess, source of life: 'Tis thine in earth's profundities to dwell, Fast by the wide and dismal gates of hell. Jove's holy offspring, of a beauteous mien, Avenging Goddess, subterranean queen.

The Furies' source, fair-hair'd, whose frame proceeds From Jove's ineffable and secret seeds. Mother of Bacchus, sonorous, divine, And many form'd, the parent of the vine. Associate of the Seasons, essence bright, All-ruling virgin, bearing heavenly light. With fruits abounding, of a bounteous mind, Horn'd, and alone desir'd by those of mortal kind. O vernal queen, whom grassy plains delight, Sweet to the smell, and pleasing to the sight: Whose holy forms in budding fruits we view, Earth's vig'rous offspring of a various hue: Espous'd in autumn, life and death alone To wretched mortals from thy pow'r is known: For thine the task, according to thy will, Life to produce, and all that lives to kill. Hear, blessed Goddess, send a rich increase Of various fruits from earth, with lovely Peace; Send Health with gentle hand, and crown my life With blest abundance, free from noisy strife; Last in extreme old age the prey of death, Dismiss me willing to the realms beneath, To thy fair palace and the blissful plains Where happy spirits dwell, and Pluto reigns.

Ninth Day. The ninth day was known as the Day of Earthen Vessels because it was the custom on that day to fill two jugs with wine, one was placed towards the east and the other towards the west, and after the repetition of certain mystical formulae both were overthrown, the wine being spilt upon the ground as a libation. The first of these formulae was directed towards the sky as a prayer for rain and the second to the earth as a prayer for fertility.

On the tenth day the majority of the people returned to their homes, with the exception of every third and fifth year, when they remained behind for the Mystery Plays and Sports which lasted from two to three days.

The ancient sanctuary in which the Mysteries were celebrated was burnt by the Persians in B. C. 480 or 479, and a new sanctuary was built, or, at least, begun under the administration of Pericles. Plutarch says that Coroebus began the Temple of Initiation at Eleusis, but only lived to finish the lower rank of columns with their architraves. Metagenes, of the ward of Xypete, added the rest of the entablature and the upper row of columns, and Xenocles of Cholargus built the dome on the top. The long wall, the building of which Socrates says he heard Pericles propose to the people, was undertaken by Callicrates. Cratinus satirised the work as proceeding very slowly:

Stone upon stone the orator has pil'd With swelling words, but words will build no walls.

In the fourth century of the Christian era the temple at Eleusis was destroyed by the Goths at the instigation of the monks who followed the hosts of Alaric.

The revenues from the celebrations must have been considerable. At both the Lesser Mysteries and the Greater Mysteries a charge of one obole a day was demanded from each one attending, which was given to the hierophant. The Hierocceryx received a half obole a day, and other assistants a similar sum.

PART III - THE ELEUSINIAN MYSTERIES - THEIR MYSTICAL SIGNIFICANCE

Life, as we know it, was looked upon by the ancient philosophers as death. Plato considered the body as the sepulchre of the soul and in the "Cratylus" acquiesces in the doctrine of Orpheus that the soul is punished through its union with the body. Empedocles, lamenting his connection with this corporeal world, pathetically exclaimed:

> For this I weep, for this indulge my woe,
> That ever my Oh such novel realms should know.

> He also calls this material abode, or the realms of generation,
> a joyless region,
> Where slaughter, rage, and countless ills reside.

Philolaus, the celebrated Pythagorean, wrote:

The ancient theologists and priests testify that the soul is united with the body for the sake of suffering punishment and that it is buried in the body as in a sepulchre while Pythagoras himself said:

Whatever we see when awake is death, and when asleep a dream.

This is the truth intended to be expressed in the Mysteries. Pindar, speaking of the Eleusinian Mysteries, says:

Blessed is he who on seeing those common concerns under the earth knows both the end of life and the given end of Jupiter.

Psyche is said to have fallen asleep in Hades through rashly attempting to behold corporeal beauty and the truth intended to be taught by the Lesser Mysteries was that prudent men who earnestly employed themselves in divine concerns were, above all others, in a vigilant state and that imprudent men who pursued objects of a different nature were asleep and only engaged in the delusions of dreams and if they happened to die in this sleep before they were aroused they would be afflicted with similar, but still sharper, visions in a future state.

Matter was regarded by the Egyptians as a certain mire or mud. They called matter the dregs or sediment of the first life. Before the first purification the candidate for initiation into the Eleusinian Mysteries was smeared with clay or mire, which it was the object of the purification to wash away. While the soul is in a state of servitude to the body it lives confined as it were in bonds through the dominion of this Titanic life. The Lesser Mysteries were intended to symbolize the condition of the soul while subservient to the body and a liberation from this servitude, through purgative virtues, was what the wisdom of the Ancients intended to signify by the descent into Hades and the speedy return from those dark abodes. They were held to contain perfective rites and appearances and the tradition of the sacred doctrines necessary to the perfection or accomplishment of the most splendid visions. The perfective part, said Proclus, precedes initiation, as initiation precedes inspection.

Dogmatic instruction was not included in the Mysteries: the doctrine of the immortality of the soul traces its origin to sources anterior to the rise of the Mysteries. At Eleusis the way was shown how to secure for the soul after death the best possible fate. The miracle of regeneration rather than the eternity of being was taught.

Plato in the seventh book of the Republic says:

He who is not able by the exercise of his reason to define the idea of the good, separating it from all other objects and piercing as in a battle through every kind of argument; endeavouring to confute, not according to opinion hut according to evidence, and proceeding with all these dialectical exercises with an unshaken reason he who cannot accomplish this, would you not say that he neither knows the good itself, nor anything which is properly demonstrated good? And would you not assert that such a one when he apprehended it rather through the medium of opinion than of science, that in the present life he is sunk in sleep and conversant with delusions and dreams; and that before he is roused to a vigilant state he will descend to Hades, and be overwhelmed with sleep perfectly profound?

Olympiodorus in this MS Commentary on the Gorgias of Plato says of the Elysian fields:

It is necessary to know that the fortunate islands are said to be raised above the sea.... Hercules is reported to have accomplished his last labor in the Hesperian regions, signifying by this that having vanquished an obscure and terrestrial life, he afterwards lived in open day, that is, in truth and resplendent light. So that he who in the present state vanquishes as much as possible a corporeal life, through the exercise of the cathartic virtues, passes in reality into the fortunate islands at the soul, and lives surrounded with the bright splendors of truth and wisdom proceeding from the sun of good.

The esoteric teaching was not, of course, grasped by all initiates: the majority merely recognized or grasped the exoteric doctrine of a future state of rewards and punishments. Virgil, in his description of the Mysteries in the Aeneid, confines himself to the exoteric teaching. Aenas having passed over the Stygian lake meets with the three-headed Celberus. By Cerberus must be understood the discriminative part of the soul, of which a dog, on account of its sagacity, is an emblem. The three heads signify the intellective, dianoetic, and doxastic powers. "He dragg'd the three mouth'd dog to upper day," i. e., by temperance, continence, and other virtues he drew upwards the various powers of the soul.

The fable of Persephone, as belonging to the Mysteries, was properly of a mixed nature, composed of all four species of fables theological, physical, animistic, and material. According to the arcana of ancient theology, the Coric order, i. e., that belonging to Persephone, is two-fold, one part supermundane and the other mundane.

Proclus says:

According to the rumor of theologists, who delivered to us the most holy Eleusinian Mysteries, Persephone abides on high, in those dwellings of her mother which she prepared for her in inaccessible places, exempt from the sensible world. But she likewise dwells with Pluto, administering terrestrial concerns, governing the recesses of the earth and imparting soul to beings which are of themselves inanimate and dead.

According to Nosselt the following may be taken as the meaning of the myth of Demeter and her lost daughter:

Persephone, the daughter of the all-productive earth (Demeter) is the seed. The earth rejoices at the sight of the plants and flowers, but they fade and wither, and the seed disappears quickly from the face of the earth when it is strewn on the ground. The dreaded monarch of the under world has taken possession of it. In vain the mother Searches for her child, the whole face of nature mourns her loss, and everything sorrows and grieves with her. But, secretly and unseen, the seed develops itself in the lap of the earth, and at length it starts forth: what was dead is now alive; the earth, all decked with fresh green, rejoices at the recovery of her long-lost daughter and everything shares in the joy.

Demeter was worshipped in a two-fold sense by the Greeks as the foundress of agriculture and as goddess of law and order. They used to celebrate yearly in her honor the Thesmophoria, or Festival of Laws.

According to Taylor, the Platonist, Demeter in the legend represents the evolution of that self-inspective part of our nature which we properly determine intellect, and Persephone that vital, self-moving, and animate part which we call soul. Pluto signifies the whole of a material nature, and, according to Pythagoras, the empire of this god commences downward from the Galaxy or Milky Way. Sallust says that among the mundane divinities Ceres is the deity of the planet Saturn. The cavern signifies the entrance into mundane life accomplished by the union of the soul with this terrestrial body. Demeter, who was afraid lest some violence be offered to Persephone on account of her inimitable beauty, conveyed her privately to Sicily and concealed her in a house built on purpose by the Cyclops while she herself directs her course to the temple of Cybele, the mother of the gods. Here we see the first cause of the soul's descent, viz., her desertion of a life wholly according to intellect, occultly signified by the separation of Persephone and Demeter. Afterwards Jupiter instructed Venus to go and betray Persephone from her retirement that Pluto might be enabled to carry her away, and, to prevent any suspicion in the virgin's mind, he commanded Diana and Pallas to bear her company. The three goddesses on arrival found Persephone at work on a scarf for her mother, on which she had embroidered the primitive chaos and the formation of the world. Venus is significant of desire, which, even in the celestial regions (for such is the residence of Persephone until she is ravished by Pluto) begins silently and fraudulently to creep into the recesses of the soul. Minerva is symbolical of the rational power of the soul; and Diana represents nature, or the merely natural and vegetable part of our composition, both ensnared through the allurements of desire.

In Ovid we have Narcissus, the metamorphosis of a youth who fell a victim to love of his own corporeal form. The rape of Persephone, according to the Homeric Hymn to Demeter, was the immediate consequence of her gathering this wonderful flower. By Narcissus falling in love with his shadow in the limpid stream we behold a beautiful representation of a soul, which, by vehemently gazing on the flowing condition of a material body, becomes enamored of a corporeal life and changed into a life consisting wholly of the mere energies of nature. Pluto, forcing his passage through the earth, seizes on Persephone and carries her away, despite the resistance of Minerva and Diana, who are forbidden by Jupiter to attempt her deliverance. This signifies that the lapse of the soul into a material nature is contrary to the genuine wish and proper condition. Pluto, having hurried Persephone into the infernal regions, marriage next succeeds. That is to say, the soul having sunk into the profoundities of a material nature, there is the union with the dark tenement of the body. Night is with great beauty and propriety introduced, standing by the nuptial couch and confirming the oblivious league. That is to say, the soul, by union with a material body, becomes familiar with darkness and subject to the empire of night, in consequence of which she dwells wholly with delusive phantoms and till she breaks her fetters is deprived of the perception of that which is real and true.

The nine days of the Festival are significant of the descent of the soul. The soul, in falling Mom her original, divine abode in the heavens, passes through eight spheres, viz., the inerratic sphere and the seven planets, assuming a different body and employing different energies in each, and finally becomes connected with the sublunary world and a terrene body on the ninth.

Demeter and the art of tillage signifies the descent of intellect into the realms of generation and becomes the greatest benefit and ornament which a material nature is capable of receiving: without the participation of intellect in the lower regions of matter nothing but an irrational soul and a brutal life would subsist.

The teaching of the Mysteries was that virtue only could entitle men to happiness and that rites, ceremonies, lustrations, and sacrifices would not supply the® want. Virgil declares that the secret of the Mysteries was the unity of the Godhead. The Mysteries declared that the after life was not necessarily or for all men the shadowy, weary existence which it had hitherto been supposed to be, but that there were rites of purification and sacrifices of a sacramental kind which gave man a better hope for the future. Thus the Eleusinian Mysteries became the chief agent in the conversion of the Greek world from the Homeric view of Hades to a more hopeful belief as to man's state after death.

Pindar says, referring to the Mysteries:

Happy is he who has seen these things before leaving this world: he realizes the beginning and the end of life, as ordained by Zeus.

Sophocles wrote:

Oh, thrice blessed the mortals, who, having contemplated these Mysteries, have descended to Hades; for those only will there be a future life of happiness the others there will find nothing but suffering.

Isocrates, in his Panegyrics, says:

Demeter, who came to our country, bestowed on us two priceless gifts, the cultivation of the fruits of the earth, which compelled us to leave our savage state; and the ceremony which brings to the initiated the sweetest consolation at death and the hope of eternity.

PART IV - THE ELEUSINIAN MYSTERIES INITIATORY RITES

Two important facts must be set down with regard to the Mysteries: first, the general custom of all Athenian citizens, and afterwards of all Greeks generally and many foreigners, to seek admission in the only possible manner, viz., by initiation; and, second, the scrupulous care exercised by the Eumo (1)pides to ensure that only persons duly qualified, of irreproachable, or at any rate, of circumspect character passed the portals. In the earlier days of the Mysteries it was a necessary condition that the candidates for initiation should be free-born Athenians, but, in course of time, this rule was relaxed, until eventually strangers and foreigners, slaves and even courtesans were admitted, on condition that they were introduced by a mystagogue, who was, of course, an Athenian. An interesting inscription was discovered a few years ago demonstrating the fact that the public slaves of the city were initiated at the public expense. Lysias was able without any difficulty to secure the initiation of his mistress Metanira, who was then in the service of the courtesan Nicareta. There always prevailed, however, the strict rule that no one could be admitted who had been guilty of murder or homicide, wilful or accidental, or who had been convicted of witchcraft, and all who had incurred the capital penalty for conspiracy or treason were also excluded. Nero sought admission into the Eleusinian Mysteries! but was rejected because of the many slaughters connected with his name Apollonius of Tyana was desirous of being admitted into the Eleusinian Mysteries, but the hierophant refused to admit him on the ground that he was a magician and had intercourse with divinities other than those of the Mysteries, declaring that he would never initiate a wizard or throw open the Mysteries to a man addicted to impure rites. Apollonius retorted: "You have not yet mentioned the chief of my offenses, which is that, knowing as I do, more about the initiatory rites than you do yourself, I have nevertheless come to you as if you were wiser than I am." The hierophant when he saw that the exclusion of Apollonius was not by any means popular with the crowd, changed his tone and said: "Be thou initiated, for thou seemest to be some wise man that has come here." But Apollonius replied: "I will be initiated at another time and it is (mentioning a name) who will initiate me." Herein, says Philostratus, he showed his gift of precision, for he glanced at the one who succeeded the hierophant he addressed and presided over the temple four years later when Apollonius was initiated.

Persons of both sexes and of all ages were initiated and neglect of the ceremony was regarded almost in the light of a crime. Socrates was reproached for being almost the only Athenian who had not applied for initiation. Persians were pointedly excluded from the ceremony. Athenians of both sexes were granted the privilege of initiation during childhood on the presentation of their father, but only the first degree of initiation was permitted. For the second and third degrees it was necessary to have arrived at full age. So great was the rush of candidates for initiation when the restrictions were relaxed that Cicero was able to write that the inhabitants of the most distant regions flocked to Eleusis in order to be initiated. Thus it became the custom with all Romans who journeyed to Athens to take advantage of the opportunity to become initiates. Even the Emperors of Rome, the official heads of the Roman religion, the masters of the world, came to the Eumolpides to proffer the request that they might receive the honor of initiation and become participants in the Sacred Mysteries revealed by the goddess.

While Augustus, who was initiated in the year B. C. 21, did not hesitate to show his antipathy towards the religion of the Egyptians, towards Judaism and Druidism, he was always scrupulous in observing the pledge of secrecy demanded of initiates into the Eleusinian Mysteries, and on one occasion, when it became necessary for some of the priests of the Eleusinian temple to proceed to Rome to plead before his tribunal on the question of privilege, and, in the course of the evidence to speak of certain ceremonial in connection with the Mysteries of which it was not lawful to speak in the presence of the uninitiated, he ordered everyone to leave the tribunal so that he and the witnesses alone remained. The Eleusinian Mysteries were not deemed inimical to the welfare of the Roman Empire as were the religions of the Egyptians, Jews, and ancient Britons.

Claudius, another imperial initiate, conceived the idea of transferring the scene of the Mysteries to Rome and, according to Suetonius, was about to put the project into execution, when it was ruled that it was obligatory that the principal scenic presentation of the Mysteries must be celebrated on the ground trodden by the feet of Demeter and where the goddess herself had ordered her temple to be erected.

The initiation of the emperor Hadrian took place in A. D. 125, when he was present at the Lesser Mysteries in the spring and at the Greater Mysteries in the following autumn. In September A. D. 129, he was again at Athens when he presented himself for the third degree, as is known from Dion Cassius, confirmed by a letter written by the Emperor himself, in which he mentions a journey from Eleusis to Ephesus made at that time. Hadrian is the only imperial initiate who persevered and passed through all three degrees. Since he remained at Eleusis as long as it was possible for him to do after the completion of his initiation it is not rash to assume that he was inspired by something more than curiosity or even a desire to show respect.

It is uncertain whether Antonin was initiated, although from an inscription it seems probable that he was and that he should be included in the list of royal initiates. Both Marcus Aurelius and Commodus, father and son, were initiated at the same time, at the Lesser Mysteries in March, A. D. 176, and at the Greater Mysteries in the following September. Septimus Severus was initiated before he ascended the throne.

There was, as stated, three degrees, and the ordinary procedure with regard to initiation was as follows:

In the flower month of spring, Anthesterion, corresponding to February-March, an applicant could, if approved, become an initiate into the first degree and participate in the Lesser Mysteries at the Eleusinion at Agra, near Athens. The ceremony of initiation into the Lesser Mysteries was much less elaborate than the ceremony of initiation into the Greater Mysteries. The candidates had to keep chaste and unpolluted for nine days prior to the ceremony, to which they came offering sacrifices and prayers and wearing crowns and garlands of flowers. Immediately prior to the celebration of the Lesser Mysteries those about to be initiated were prepared by mystagogues, the teachers selected from the families of the Eumolpides and the Keryces, and instructed in the story of Demeter and Persephone, the character of the purification necessary and the preparatory rites, the fast days, with particulars of what food could and must not be eaten, and the numerous sacrifices to be offered up under the direction of the mystagogues. Without this preparation no one could be admitted to the Mysteries. There was, however, neither secret doctrine nor dogmatic teaching in the instruction given. Revelation came through contemplation of the sacred objects displayed by the hierophant, and by the communication of mystic formulae; but the preparation demanded of the initiates, the secrecy imposed, the ceremonies at which they assisted in the dead silence of the night created a strong impression and lively hope in regard to the future life. No other cult in Greece, still less the cold Roman religion, had anything of the kind to offer. In fasting from food and drink before and after initiation the candidates attached to this voluntary privation no idea of maceration or expiation of faults: it was simply the reproduction of an event in the life of the goddess Demeter. Purity was an indispensable condition for all who would enter the temples. Bowls or vases of consecrated or holy water were placed at the entrance for the purposes of aspersion. In cases of special impurity a delay of one or more days in the preparation became necessary and unctions of oil or repeated immersions in water were administered. In the preparation of candidates for initiation, purification assumed an exceptional importance. Hence several writers have maintained that the primary aim of initiation was the acquirement of moral purity. The outward physical purity, the result of immersion prior to initiation, was but the symbol of the inward purity which should result from initiation. The duty of the mystagogues was to see that the candidates were in a state of physical cleanliness and to see that that condition was maintained throughout the ceremony. According to the inscriptions there appear to have been temples or buildings set apart for the cleansing of candidates from special impurities. After initiation into the Lesser Mysteries the neophyte was permitted to go as far as the outer vestibule of the temple. In the following autumn, if of full age, he could be initiated into the Greater Mysteries, into the second degree, that of mysta. This, however, did not entitle the recipients of that honor to join in all the acts of worship or to witness the whole of the ceremonial at Eleusis. A further year had to elapse before the third degree could be taken, before they could become epoptae, and see with their own eyes and hear with their own ears the whole of the Greater Mysteries. The Lesser Mysteries were celebrated at Athens on the hill of Agra, to the right of the Stadium in a temple dedicated to Demeter and Persephone. Occasionally when the number of candidates was very large the Lesser Mysteries were celebrated twice in the year in order to give those too late for the ceremony in Anthesterion another opportunity before the Greater Mysteries were held.

At the next celebration of the Greater Mysteries, after having sacrificed to Demeter, the initiate received the second degree and became numbered among the mystae. The preliminary to this degree was bathing in the river Ilissus, after which the Daduchos instructed each candidate to place the left foot on the skin of an animal which had been sacrificed to Zeus, in which position the oath of secrecy was taken. Jevons, in his Introduction to the Study of Religion, says that no oath was demanded of the initiated but that silence was observed generally as an act of reverence rather than as an act of purposed concealment. There seems, however, to be conclusive evidence that an oath of secrecy was demanded and taken, at any rate, in the second and third degrees, if not in the first. Moreover, there are on record several prosecutions of citizens for having broken the pledge of secrecy they had given. Aeschylus was indicted for having disclosed in the theatre certain details of the Mysteries, and he only escaped punishment by proving that he had never been initiated and could not therefore have violated any obligation of secrecy. A Greek scholar says that in five of his tragedies Aeschylus spoke of Demeter and therefore may be supposed in these cases to have touched upon subjects connected with the Mysteries; and Heraclides of Pontus says that on this account he was in danger of being killed by the populace if he had not fled for refuge to the altar of Dionysos and then begged off by the Areopagites and acquitted on the ground of his exploits at Marathon. An accusation was brought against Aristotle of having performed a funeral sacrifice in honor of his wife in imitation of the Eleusinian ceremonies. Alcibiades was charged with mimicking the sacred Mysteries in one of his drunken revels, when he represented the hierophant; Theodorus, one of his friends, represented the herald; and another, Polytion, that of the torch- bearer; the other companions attending as initiates and being addressed as Mystae. The information against him ran:

Thessalus, the son of Cimon, of the ward of Laeais, accuseth Aleibiades, the son of Clinias, of the ward of Seambonis, of sacrilegiously offending the goddess Ceres and her daughter Persephone by counterfeiting their Mysteries and shewing them to his companions in his own house, wearing such a robe as the high priest does when he shows the holy things; he called himself high priest, as did Polytion, torch-bearer; and Theodorus, of the ward of Phygea, herald; and the rest of his companions he called persons initiated and

Brethren of the Secret; therein acting contrary to the rules and ceremonies established by the Eumolpides, the heralds and priests at Eleusis.

Alcibiades did not appear in answer to the charge, was condemned in his absence and his goods were confiscated. There was quite a panic about this time B. C. 415. Many prominent citizens, Andocides included, were prosecuted. He was included in the indictment against Alcibiades. "This man," said his accuser, "vested in the same costume as a hierophant, has shown the sacred objects to men who were not initiated and has uttered words it is not permissible to repeat." Andocides admitted the charge, turned king's evidence, and named himself and certain others as the culprits. He was rewarded with a free pardon under a decree which Isotmides had issued but those whom he named were put to death or outlawed and their goods confiscated. Andocides afterwards entered the temple and was charged with breaking the law in so doing. He defended himself before a court of heliasts, all of whom had been initiated into the Mysteries, the president of the Court being the Archon Basileus. The indictment was lodged by Cephisius, the chief prosecutor, with the Archon Basileus during the celebration of the Greater Mysteries, when Andocides was at Eleusis. He was acquitted and it is asserted that Cephisius failed to obtain one-fifth of the votes of the Court, the consequence being that he had to pay a fine of 1,000 drachmae and to suffer permanent exclusion from the Eleusinian shrine.

Diagiras was accused of railing at the sanctity of the Mysteries of Eleusis in such a manner as to deter persons from seeking initiation and a reward of one talent was offered to any one who should kill him or two talents to anyone who should bring him alive.

An ancient theme of oratorical composition and one set even in the sixth century of the Christian era was:

The law punishes with death whoever has disclosed the Mysteries: some one to whom the initiation has been revealed in a dream asks one of the initiated if what he has seen is in conformity with reality: the initiate acquiesces by a movement of the head: and for that he is accused of impiety.

Every care, therefore, was taken to prevent the secrecy of the Mysteries from becoming known to all save initiates. They have, however, come to light in a great measure through the ancient writings and inscriptions. Step by step and piece by piece the diligent researcher has been rewarded by the discovery of disconnected and isolated fragments which, by themselves, supply no precise information, but, taken in the aggregate, form a perfect mosaic. Though it was strictly forbidden to reveal what took place within the sacred enclosure and in the Hall of Initiation it was permissible to state clearly the object of initiation and the advantages to be derived from the act. Not only was the breaking of the pledge of secrecy given by an initiate visited with severe, sometimes even capital, punishment, but the forcing of the temple enclosure by the uninitiated, as happened sometimes, was an offence of equally heinous character. By virtue of the unwritten laws and customs dating back to the most remote periods the penalty of death was frequently pronounced for faults not grave in themselves, but solely because they concerned religion. It was probably by virtue of those unwritten laws that the priests ordered the death of two young Arcanians who had penetrated, through ignorance, into the sacred precincts. This was in B. C. 200 and Rome made war upon Philip V of Macedonia on the complaint of the government of Athens against that king who wished to punish them for having rigorously applied the ancient laws to those two offenders, who were found guilty of entering the sanctuary at Eleusis, they not having been initiated. No judicial penalty, however, was meted out to the fanatical Epicurean eunuch, who, with the object of proving that the gods had no existence forced himself blaspheming into that part of the sanctuary into which the hierophant and hierophantide alone had the right of entry. Aelianus states that a divine punishment in the form of a disease alone overtook him. Horace declared that he would not risk his life by going on the water with a companion who had revealed the secret of the Mysteries.

One of the essential preliminaries to initiation into each degree was fasting. Two days prior to initiation into the second and third degrees were spent by the candidate in solitary retirement when a strict fast was observed. It was a "retreat" in the strictest sense of the word. Fasting was practised, not only in imitation of the sufferings of Demeter when searching for Persephone, but because of the danger of the contact of holy things with unholy, the clean with the unclean. Thus it was held that even to speak of the Mysteries to the uninitiated would be as dangerous as to allow such unclean persons to take part in the ceremonies. Hence the punishment meted out by the State was in lieu of, or to avert, the divine wrath which such pollution might bring on the community at large. At the entrance to the temple tablets were placed containing a list of forbidden foods. The list included several kinds of fish, including the whistle-fish, gurnet, crab and mullet. The whistle- fish and crab were held to be impure, the first because it laid its eggs through the mouth and the second because it ate filth which other fish rejected. The gurnet was rejected because of its fecundity as witnessed in its annual triple laying of eggs, but, according to some writers, it was rejected because it ate a fish which was poisonous to mankind. It is believed that other fish were forbidden but Prophyry was probably exaggerating when he says that all fish were interdicted. Birds bred at home, such as chickens and pigeons, were also on the banned list as were beans and certain vegetables which were forbidden for a mystic reason which Pausanias said he dared not reveal save to the initiated. The probable reason was that they were connected in some way with the wanderings of Demeter. Pomegranates were, of course, forbidden from the incident of the eating of the pomegranate seeds by Persephone.

The candidates were carefully instructed in these rules beforehand. Originally the instruction of the candidates was in the hands of the hierophant, who, following the example of his ancestor, Eumolpus, claimed the privilege of preparing the candidates as well as that of communicating to them the divine Mysteries. But the constantly increasing number of applicants made it necessary to employ auxiliary instructors, and this work was given over to the charge of the mystagogues, who prepared either one individual or a group of candidates, the hierophant reserving to himself the general direction of the instruction. In the course of the initiation ceremony certain words had to be spoken by the candidates and these were made known to them in advance, although, of course, apart from their context.

Admission to the second degree took place during the night between the sixth and seventh days of the celebration of the Mysteries, when they were led into the temple precincts and the second Archon opened the ceremony with prayers and sacrifices. The candidates were crowned with myrtle and on entering the building an edifice so vast and capacious as to exceed in area the largest theatre of the period they purified themselves by immersing their hands in the consecrated water. The priests, vested in their sacerdotal garments, then came forward. During the first part of the ceremony the candidates were assembled in the outer hall of the temple, the temple proper being closed. Then a herald came forth and proclaimed: "Away from here all ye that are not purified, and whose souls have not been freed from sin." If any who were not votaries had by chance entered the precincts they now left for if discovered afterwards the punishment was death. In order to make certain that no intruders remained behind all who were present had to answer certain specified questions. Then all again immersed their hands in the consecrated water and renewed the pledge of secrecy. Next they took off their ordinary garments, and girded themselves with the skins of young does, whereupon the priests wished them joy of all the happiness their initiation would bring them and then went away. Within a few minutes the building was plunged in total darkness. Suddenly terrific peals of thunder resounded, shaking the very foundations of the temple; vivid flashes of lightning lit up the darkness and displayed fearful forms, while dreadful sighs, groans, and cries of pain resounded on all sides, like the shrieks of the condemned in Tartarus. The novices were taken hold of by invisible hands, their hair was torn, and they were beaten and thrown to the ground. At last a faint light became visible in the distance and a fearful scene appeared before their eyes. The gates of Tartarus were opened and the abode of the condemned lay before them. They could hear the cries of anguish and the vain regrets of those to whom Paradise was lost forever and could, moreover, witness their hopeless remorse. They saw, as well as heard, all the tortures of the condemned. The Furies, armed with relentless scourges and flaming torches, drove the unhappy victims incessantly to and fro, never letting them rest for a moment. Meanwhile the loud voices of the hierophant, who represented the judge of the world, was heard expounding the meaning of what was passing before them and warning and threatening the initiates. It may well be imagined that all these fearful scenes were so terrifying that very frequently beads of anguish appeared on the brows of the novices. At length the gates of Tartarus closed and the innermost sanctuary of the temple lay open before the initiates in dazzling light. In the midst stood the statue of the goddess Demeter brilliantly decked and gleaming with precious stones; heavenly music entranced their souls; a cloudless sky overshadowed them; fragrant perfumes arose; and in the distance the privileged spectators beheld flowering meads, where the blessed danced and amused themselves with innocent games and pastimes. Among others writers the scene is described by Aristophanes in The Frogs:

Heracles: The voyage is a long one. For you will come directly to a very big lake of abysmal depth.

Dionysos: Then how shall I get taken across it?

Heracles: In a little boat just so big; an old man who plies the boat will take you across for a fee of two oboles.

Dionysos: Oh dear! How very powerful those two oboles are all over the world. How did they manage to get here?

Heracles: Theseus brought them. After this you will see serpents and wild beasts in countless numbers and very terrible. Then a great slough and over-flowing dung; and in this you'll see lying anyone who ever yet at any place wronged his guest or beat his mother, or smote his father's jaw, or swore an oath and foreswore himself.... And next a breathing of flutes shall be wafted around you, and you shall see a very beautiful light, even as in this world, and myrtle groves, and happy choirs of men and women, and a loud clapping of hands.

Dionysos: And who are these people, pray?

Heracles: The initiated. It was regarded as permissible to describe the scenes of the initiation, and this has been done by many writers, but a complete silence was demanded as to the means employed to realize the end, the rites and ceremonies in which the initiate took part, the emblems which were displayed, and the actual words uttered and the slightest divergence rendered the offender liable to the strongest possible condemnation and chastisement.

In the course of the ceremony the hierophant asked a series of questions to which written answers had been prepared and committed to memory by the candidates. Holy Mysteries were revealed to the initiates from a book called Petroma, a word derived from petra, a stone, and so called because the writings were kept enclosed between two cemented stones. The garments worn by the candidates during the initiation ceremony were accounted sacred, and equal with incantations and consecrated charms in their power to avert evils. Consequently, they were never cast off until torn and tattered. Nor was it usual, even then, to throw them away but it was customary to make them into twaddling clothes for children or to consecrate them to Demeter and Persephone.

Admission to the third degree took place during the night between the seventh and eighth days of the celebration of the Mysteries. This, the final degree with the exception of those called to be hierophants, was known as the degree of epoptie. Exactly in what the ceremonial consisted, save in one particular presently to be described, little is known. Hippolytus is practically the only authority for the main incident of the degree. Certain words and signs were communicated to the initiated which, when pronounced after death, were held to ensure the eternal happiness of the soul.

The most solemn part of the ceremony was that which has been described by some writers as the hierogamy or sacred marriage of Zeus and Demeter, although some have mistakenly referred to it as the marriage of Pluto and Proserphine. During the celebration of the Mysteries the hierophant and the hierophantide descended into a cave or deep recess and, after remaining there for a time, returned to the assembly, surrounded seemingly by flames, the hierophant displaying to the gaze of the initiated an ear of corn and exclaiming in a loud voice: "The divine Brimo has Wiven birth to the holy child Brimos: the strong has Drought forth strength."

"The Athenians," says Hippolytus, "in the initiation of Eleusis show to the epoptes the great, admirable, and most perfect mystery of the epoptie: an ear of corn gathered in silence." The statement is so clear as to leave no doubt whatever on the subject; indeed, it has never been called into question. The presentation of the ear of corn was part of the Mysteries of Eleusis and it was reserved for the epoptes.

Much has been made of this incident by many who can see no beauty in pre-Christian or non-Christian forms of religion, their comments being based mainly on a statement of St. Gregory Nazianus, who stands alone in discerning lewdness in the Eleusinian ceremonial. He says:

It is not in our religion that you will find a seduced Cora, a wandering Demeter, a Keleos, and a Triptolemos appearing with serpents; that Demeter is capable of certain acts and that she permits others. I am really ashamed to throw light on the nocturnal orgies of the initiations. Eleusis knows as well as the witnesses the secret of this spectacle, which is with reason kept so profound.

Apart from this isolated statement the Eleusinian Mysteries have not been charged as many ancient rites were with promoting immorality. In his account of the doings of the false prophet Alexander of Abountichos, Lucian describes how the impostor instituted rites which were a close parody of those at Eleusis and he narrates the details of the travesty. Among the mimetic performances were not only the Epiphany and birth of a god but the enactment of a sacred marriage. All preliminaries were gone through and Lucian says that but for the abundance of lighted torches the marriage would actually have been consummated. The part of the hierophant was taken-by the false prophet himself. From the travesty it is evident that in the genuine Mysteries in silence, in darkness, and in perfect chastity the sacred marriage was enacted and that immediately afterwards the hierophant came forth and standing in a blaze of torchlight made the announcement to the initiates. 'When came the words from the hierophant:

I have tasted, I have drunk "cyceon." I have taken from the cystus and after having tasted of it I placed it in the calathos. I again took it from the calathos and put it back in the cistus.

This formula, notwithstanding its length, became the "pass word" of the perfect initiate.

Dr. Jevons maintains that this ear of corn was the totem of Eleusis and this view has been adopted by M. Reinach who says:

We find in the texts a certain trace not only of the cult but of the adoration and the exaltation (in the Christian meaning of the word) of the ear of corn.

But he has omitted to quote the texts on which he relies for this assertion. It would be interesting to know why among all the plants which die and revive in the course of a year, wheat was chosen for preference, why the ear more than the grain, why it should be emphasized that it was gathered, for what reason the spectacle was reserved for the epoptae and in what manner it secures or ensures for the individual a blissful existence after death. The demonstration presupposes that the preceding rites and ceremonies were leading up to this supreme display. This practically ended the third degree save that then the epoptae were placed upon exalted seats around which the priests circled in mystic dances. The day succeeding admission into the final degree was regarded as a rigorous fast at the conclusion of which the epoptae also drank of the mystic kukeon and ate of the sacred cakes.

The Greeks laid great stress upon the advantages to be derived from initiation. Not only were the initiates under the protection of the State but the very act of initiation was said to assist in the spreading of good will among men, keep the soul free from sin and crime, place men under the special protection of the gods, and provide them with the means of attaining perfect virtue, the power of living a spotless life, and assure them of a peaceful death and everlasting bliss hereafter. The priests assured all who participated in the Mysteries that they would have a higher place in Elysium, a clearer understanding, and a more intimate intercourse with the gods, whereas the uninitiated would always remain in outer darkness. Indeed, in the final degree the epoptae were said to be admitted to the presence of and converse with the goddesses Demeter and Persephone. Initiates were placed under the immediate care and protection of the goddess Demeter. Initiation was referred to frequently as a guarantee of salvation conferred by outward and visible signs and by sacred formulae.

According to Theo of Smyrna the full or complete initiation consisted of five steps or degrees:

Again, philosophy may be called the initiation into true sacred ceremonies, and the tradition of genuine mysteries; for there are five parts of initiation; the first of which is previous purgation; for neither are the Mysteries communicated to all who are willing to receive them, but there are certain characters who are prevented by the voice of the crier, such as those who possess impure hands and an articulate voice, since it is necessary that such as are not expelled from the Mysteries should first be refined by certain purgations, hut after purgation the tradition of the sacred rite succeeds. The third part is denominated inspection. And the fourth which is the end and design of inspection is the binding of the head and fixing the crown: so that the initiated may, by this means, he enabled to communicate to others the sacred rites in which he has been instructed; whether after this he becomes a torchbearer, or an interpreter of the Mysteries, or sustains some other part of the sacerdotal office. But the fifth which is produced from all these, is friendship with divinity, and the enjoyment of that felicity which arises from intimate converse with the gods. According to Plato purification is to be derived from the five mathematical disciplines, viz., arithmetic, geometry, steretometry, music, and astronomy.

The fee for initiation was a minimum sum of fifteen drachmas, in addition to which there were the usual honoraria to be bestowed towards the various officiating ministers to which reference has already been made. Presumably, also, gifts in kind were made annually to the principal clergy for an inscription of the fifth century B. C. found at Eleusis reads:

Let the hierophant and the torch-bearer command that at the mysteries the Hellenes shall offer first-fruits of their crops in accordance with ancestral usage.... To those who do these things there shall be many good things, both good and abundant crops, whoever of them do not injure the Athenians, nor the city of Athens, nor the two goddesses.

The Telestrion or Hall of Initiation, sometimes called "The Mystic Temple," was a large, covered building, about 170 feet square. It was surrounded on all sides by steps which presumably served as seats for the initiated while the sacred dramas and processions took place on the floor of the hall. These steps were partly built up and partly cut in the solid rock: in latter times they appear to have been covered with marble. There were two doors on each side of the hall with the exception of the north-west where the entrance was cut out of the solid rock, a rock terrace at a higher level adjoining it. This was probably the station of those not yet admitted to full initiation. The roof of the hall was carried by rows of columns which were more than once renewed. The Hall itself did not accommodate more than 4,000 people. The building was, perhaps, more accurately designed by Aristophanes as "The house that welcomed the mystae." Strabo's phrase for it was "The holy enclosure of the mystae" and he carefully distinguishes it from the temple of Demeter. It was not the dwelling place of any god and, therefore, contained no holy image. It was built for the celebration of a definite ritual and the Eleusinian Hall of Initiation was therefore the only known church of antiquity if by that term we understand the meeting place of the congregation.

The Religion of Robert Burns
Gilbert Patten Brown

All men possess some real worth. Creed is an invention of man. Genius is a gift of God to man. The very name "genius" signifies original, unacquired gifts, born gifts: from the Latin of Gignor, to be born; or, older still, from the Greek of Gennao, to generate, to produce. A man may be a good historian, a grammarian, or a commentator: only a man of genius can be a painter, a statuary, or a poet. The poet is an original thinker. Whenever we find a man of rare intellect working out his own destiny, and showing himself mighty among his contemporaries, we are benefited by having come in contact with such a person. In one of that type is a fineness of nature. He is usually a seer. They have lived in all ages and have been found among all races of men. They belong to no particular class or creed and are usually deeply religious in their own way of reasoning. The gentleman of this monograph is without question Scotland's greatest son. He taught the world through his poems the difference between religion and creed.

> *"The rank is but the guinea's stamp*
> *The man's the gowd for a' that."*

Possibly no poet ever lived who possessed that original style and uniqueness of composition as Robert Burns, whose eyes first saw the light of this world on the twenty-fifth day of the rough old warrior January, 1759, in the quaint little village of Alloway. The cottage, under whose historic roof he was born, is still standing. The old parish books of records, dimmed with age, show his ancestry to have been of the best blood of Ayr and Alloway. The following is a brief account of this old (Celt) family: "Lawful son of William Burns of Alloway and Agnes Brown, his spouse," and "baptized by Mr. William Dalrymple: witnesses, John Tement and James Young."

MADE A MASON

The youthful days of Burns were spent amid rural surroundings, thus giving his young brain an opportunity to read of the phi-

138

losophy of life from the open pages of the book of nature. His play-mate in school was his modest brother Gilbert. The poet's maternal grandfather, Gilbert Brown, was a farmer, and known for his upright living, also his deep religious convictions. He differed from the creed of his forefathers as did the poet. Before arriving at manhood Burns became firmly grounded in the faith of "the fatherhood of God and the brotherhood of man." While a youth he had witnessed a funeral as conducted by the institution of Masonry. That sight he had never forgot. In beauteous Tarbolton, Ayrshire, was St. David's Lodge, No. 174, whose membership consisted of the "substantial, upright, and honest gentlemen" of the neighborhood. An extract from the pages of records of that historic body, under the date of July 4, 1784, reads,-

"Robert Burns in Lockly was entered an apprentice." Signed, "R. Norman." And, under the date of October 1, the record reads, "Robert Burns in Lockly was passed and raised, Henry Cowan being Worshipful Master, James Humphrey being Senior Warden, and Alex Smith, Junior; Robert Wadrown, Secretary, and John Manson, Trea-surer; John Tammock, Tyler, and others of the brethren being present."

MORE LIGHT IN MASONRY

Robert Burns became extremely interested in his new and most fraternal home. The lessons he had learned therein had a very wel-come place in his heart, and in a short time he wished for "more light in Freemasonry," by being made a regular "Royal Arch Mason." In due season he made application for further advancement in the an-cient mysteries of the Institution. It is by the aid of the minutes of the old "record book" of "St. Abb's Lodge" of Leymouth, and under the date of May 19, 1787, that the author is able to give the following to his fraternal readers:-

"At a general encampment of St. Abb's Lodge, the following brethren were made Royal Arch Masons: Robert Burns, from the Lodge of St. James, Tarbolton, Ayrshire; and Robert Ainslie, from the Lodge of St. Luke, Edinburgh. Robert Ainslie paid one guinea admission dues; but, on account of Robert Burns' remarkable poetical genius the encampment agreed to admit him gratis, and considered them-selves honored by having a man of such shining abilities for one of their companions."

Previous to Robert Burns being made a Master Mason, St. David's Lodge, No. 174, and St. James' Lodge were consolidated under the name, "St. David's Lodge, No. 174, Ancient Freemasons," and later separated, each Lodge claiming their pride, "Bobbie" Burns, to hold membership therein.

Throughout Scotland the 24th of June is generally observed by the Masonic fraternity. In 1786 and in the early part of June, Brother Burns, being somewhat anxious to have a large attendance on the 24th (St John's Day), sent to his brother Mason, the Dr. John Mackenzie, a beautiful notice in poem form. It pleased its readers.

THE MASTER'S APRON

The attendance on that "St. John's Day" was large at renowned St. David's Lodge, and a more proud Freemason never stood in Masonic cloth than Robert Burns as he extended the warm hand of friendship and brotherhood upon that occasion. He was a frequent and most welcome visitor to Masonic meetings in many places of "Bonnie" Scotland. The following is from his talented pen:-

"There's many a badge that's unco braw
Wi' ribbons, lace, and tape on:
Let Kings and Princes wear them a'
Gie me the Master's apron
The honest craftsman's apron
The jolly Freemason's apron,
Bide he at hame, or roam afar
Before his touch fa's bolt an' bar,
The gates of fortune fly ajar,
'Gin he wears the apron.
For w'alth and honor, pride and power
Are crumbling stanes to base on:
Fraternity should rule the hour
And ilka worthy Mason,
Each free accepted Mason
Each ancient crafted Mason.
Then, brithers, let a halesome sang
Arise your friendly ranks alang.
Gude Wives and bairnes blithely sing

Ti' the ancient badge wi' the apron string
That is worn by the Maste Mason."

Our own William Cullen Bryant in his address at the Burns birthday centennial festival, Astor House, Nevi York, Jan. 25, 1859, spoke at length on Burns. The following is but a brief extract from his well-timed remarks:-

"Well has our great poet deserved this universal commemoration, for who has written like him ? What poem descriptive of rural manners and virtues, rural life in its simplicity and dignity, — yet without single false outline or touch of false coloring, — clings to our memories and lives in our bosoms like his 'Cotter's Saturday Night'? What humorous narrative in verse can be compared with his 'Tam O'Shanter'? From the fall of Adam to his time, I believe, there was nothing written in the vein of his 'Mountain Daisy': others have caught his spirit from that poem, but who among then, all excelled him? Of all the convivial songs I have ever seen in any language there is none so overflowing with the spirit of conviviality, so joyous, so contagious as his song of 'Willie brewed a Peck o' Maut.' What love songs are sweeter and tenderer than those of Burns? What song addresses itself so movingly to our love of old friends and our pleasant recollection of old days as his 'Auld Lang Syne,' or to the domestic affections so powerfully as his 'John Anderson'"?

The religion of Burns was truly the religion of a poet. "An irreligious poet is a monster," he said. "I despise the religion of a fanatic, but I love the religion of a man." So advanced has become the age of reason that these words alone make Burns mighty among the world's greatest philosophers. A true poet is a religious man. He sees goodness in all things: the works of Deity are to him ever visible.

SECTARIANISM

Years ago Scotland alone celebrated the birthday of Burns; but today people of many races, creeds, and tongues hold services commemorating that eventful day. We find many preachers of today laying their sacrifice of praise on the sacred altar of his cherished memory. Even the creed egoist or the race despot cares not to make war upon the name of Robert Burns. Form to him was nothing, sect had no welcome in his heart. The peddling politicians of sectarianism played upon his tender feelings, and, while he was yet young, forced him into arguments upon theological lines. In later years he frequently declared to the effect that the theological brawlings of his early life were not to be counted against him as hostile to religion. For true religion his respect was marked. See his philosophy in these lines, —

> *"In ploughman phrase, God send you speed,*
> *Still daily to grow wiser;*
> *And may ye better reck the rede*
> *Than ever did th' adviser."*

He wore no commercial smile, nor did he frown upon the riches of others. He was never known to speak disrespectfully of Jesus of Nazareth.

The following four lines are but a fragment of his poem as paralleled by him to the eighth chapter of John:-

> *"Then gently scan your brother man,*
> *Still gentler sister woman;*
> *Tho' they may gang a kennin' wrang,*
> *To step aside is human."*

For the sake of the songs of Burns the rational world has forgiven his sins.

Robert Burns died July 21, 1796, and was buried five days later at Alloway Kirk, Ayr. No grave in all Scotland is more cherished by the visitor than that of Robert Burns, who had many faults and who like all men made many mistakes in life, but whose tender heart gave to humanity some of the sweetest messages since the Sermon on the Mount, and whose name will live as long as biography has a charm for the children of men.

THE SWEET SINGER

Thus do we find Robert Burns to have been a very religious man. Many of his poems are sermons worthy to be cherished by all lovers of literary worth. He frowned upon no man for his form of worship of the Deity. He despised the selfishness of man in commercial life: —

"The poor, oppressed, honest man
Had never sure been born
Had there not been some recompense
To comfort those that mourn."

Again he says, —

"Great Nature spoke, with benign
'Go on, ye human race
This lower world I you resign
Be faithful and increase.' "

To the memory of his daughter who died in 1795 he wrote two verses, one of which is as follows: —

"To those who for her loss are grieved,
This consolation's given:
She's from a world of woe relieved
And blooms a rose in heaven."

One of his truest friends was John Bushby, who was known for his faith in God and his honesty of purpose in worldly affairs. At his grave Burns wrote: —

"Here lies John Bushby, honest man!
Cheat him, Devil, if you can."

"Burns' Day," January 25th, is becoming a popular day of celebration, when, by those who love the tender side of humanity, race and creed are forgotten.

Notes on the Early History of Masonic Ranks

Sir Frederick Pollock

I. THE NATURE OF THE INQUIRY

All brethren who have paid any attention to the early history of the craft are aware that our present ceremonial, while it embodies archaic features easily recognized by any one moderately acquainted with medieval language and formulas, and such as no eighteenth century antiquary could have interpolated, is in its form and order the work of the founders of the Grand Lodge Of England and their successors down to the union of the rival Grand Lodges in 1813. It is certain that its framers from Anderson and Desaguliers to Preston recast and greatly amplified their materials. We do not know fully what those materials were; indeed Anderson, who was anything but a critical antiquary, seems to have wilfully thrown a cloud of obscurity round his operations; nor is credulity the worst that has to be laid to his charge. Accordingly, so far as any direct evidence goes, it is very possible to entertain the gravest doubts as to the authenticity not only of Anderson's superstructure but of his foundations. These doubts have been carried by some learned brethren to the length of maintaining that superiority of the Master to the Fellow Craft is a pure invention or misconception void of historical warrant in the practice of the old operative lodges. With great respect for the much needed and excellent critical work of those brethren - it is enough to name Gould, Hughan, Speth, Chetwode Crawley, last but not least Dr. Fort Newton, and Dr. Hammond the accomplished librarian of the Grand Lodge of England, who are still with us - I cannot follow them to that length, and shall try to show cause for holding that there was an element of genuine restoration - restoration to be distinguished from unbroken continuity, but not merely fictitious - in the eighteenth century fabric of speculative Masonry. That Anderson and Desaguliers did not find three degrees existing in practice at the beginning of the eighteenth century may be taken as established: the only arguable question is whether we shall speak of two or one. But it is another thing to deny that there had ever been three ranks in operative Masonry; whether properly called degrees or not, is a minor question. So far as I know the word "degree" does not occur as a regular term in any of the earlier documents.

I shall not enter on detailed criticism of previous opinions, which would only make a tedious and intricate discussion, but give my own view of the evidence on the principle of trying to establish fixed points by the use of the best available means, and not attempting to reconcile the variations or Contradictions that occur in sources of inferior authority. This method, I believe, gives the best chance of finding useful clues when one is confronted with a tangle material in which the sound and the unsound seem at first hopelessly mixed. At least it will enable me to follow the order of time without perplexing digressions. We have to look for indications leading to conclusions or a choice of plausible opinions on the following points. What were the recognized ranks in medieval operative Masonry? How were they acquired or conferred? How far were the distinctions observed in practice in the time of transition from operative to speculative lodges? In the absence of any central authority we must not expect, in any case, to find complete uniformity. Medieval institutions of all kinds, it may be added, are full of exceptions and anomalies; one quite common note of the antiquarian (or otherwise interested) falsifier is that he makes things too neat and complete.

II. THE COMACINE MASTERS

In the course of the last twenty years attention has been called to the importance of the Lombard association of builder-architects (not an ordinary trade gild) known as the Comacine Masters. The recognition of their special standing as independent of any local regulations, and their influence on the general development of European architecture in the Middle Ages, may be taken as proved. It is not to my present purpose to touch on more or less plausible conjectures as to their remote antecedents and possible connection with Eastern traditions. What concerns us here is the fact that the magistri Comacini claimed and exercised a cosmopolitan privilege very like that of the Masters or Doctors of medieval universities, namely the right of both practising and teaching their art anywhere. There is no authentic evidence of any express imperial or papal grant of any such privilege, but in the Middle Ages custom and repute would for most working purposes do as well as formal title, the notion of possession with its highly important juridical consequences being extended to usage of all kinds. The University of Oxford had nothing else to rely on for its authority to confer degrees; and in the craft itself we have the "time immemorial" lodges. Now the analogy of university degrees to the ranks established in the Comacine fellowship demands a word of special notice; I do not think it can be accidental: In the Comacine ranks we find the three grades of novices or apprentices, operatori or craftsmen, and magistri. Brethren will remember that at this day the F.C. is still formally exhorted to study the liberal arts and sciences - the medieval trivium and quadrivium and the M.M. to assist and instruct the Brethren in inferior degrees. The parallel to university ranks is exact. We have in the medieval university system, especially in its English form, the commencing student or undergraduate (a convenient English term lacking a Continental equivalent) who is a member of the body but a mere learner under constant discipline, having only inchoate rights of promotion on satisfying the proper tests; then the bachelor of arts, recognized as proficient to a certain extent, and with a limited authority to teach, but still learning and not released from discipline (in statu pupillari); and lastly the master of arts or doctor, (for down to the fifteenth century these titles were equivalent) who is not only qualified to teach but bound to teach and preside as "regent" at disputations for a certain time. Traces of the distinction between "regent" and "non-regent" M.A.'s survived in England till our own days. The essence of the master's or doctor's degree was license to teach in any recognized university; whether any or how many students would come to be taught being a matter dependent on the master's own ability. In like manner the Master Mason was free, in the operative period, to undertake a contract and form a working lodge to execute it. In the fully developed university system of the later Middle Ages, now most nearly preserved in England, the doctor's degree belonged only to the superior faculties of theology, medicine and law. (The Faculty of Letters is a creation of our own time, and music is on a rather different footing). It would be fanciful to seek for any real analogy between the faculties outside Arts and the Masonic or quasi-Masonic orders and degrees outside ancient craft Masonry; but it seems worth remark that in the majority of European universities there has been a dislocation and consolidation of degrees curiously like that of which we have indications in the later operative Masonry, the faculty of Arts having made its mastership a doctorate under the name of Doctor of Philosophy, and the bachelor's degree having atrophied or never been fully established. The preliminary point I am here making is that the general idea of three ranks, namely, novice, worker still under instruction, and master giving instruction, is no modern invention but rooted in authoritative medieval tradition.

It is certain that Italian master-builders came to England at the very beginning of the Middle Ages; it is a safe inference that they brought the Comacine tradition, as there is positive architectural evidence that they brought Comacine symbolism with them; and no one acquainted with the wide and rapid spread of medieval institutions and forms by direct imitation (in the universities, again, as much as anywhere, also in municipal and other customary rules) will hesitate to believe that they found imitators. The later importation of Italian masters and artificers towards the end of the fifteenth century was of a different kind, and is not to the purpose here. We are now ready to proceed to the evidence found in English documents. I may premise that I take no notice of modern publications purporting to reproduce ancient texts or give the substance of ancient materials, but having no authentic history, coming from no proper custody, and lacking corroboration from more trustworthy sources. Happening to be rather familiar with documents of that kind in the medieval history of English law, I am clearly of opinion that even so far as there is nothing extravagantly improbable in their contents it is unsafe to treat them as historical proof of anything. One cannot so much as infer from them what was current belief or tradition at the time when they were written; for they may represent nothing but the conjecture or invention of some eccentric writer who was wilfully manufacturing evidence in support of his peculiar views. It is an elementary caution that any copy of a alleged original which fails to account for that original, or even gives a false account, must be regarded with the gravest suspicion, a suspicion not to be removed by the matter being on the face of it consistent with genuineness, if it is so. Many forgeries have been very plausible; and interpolations in copies or reconstructions of perished or lost genuine documents may give much trouble, and on the whole have given more than downright forgery. The fact that a copy comes from proper custody (such as, to take the simplest case, the place where the missing original or an official duplicate ought to have been) is a reason for giving it faith and credit, but unfortunately not a conclusive reason.

III. OPERATIVE MASTER MASONS

Let us begin with a class of testimony which is undesigned, authentic and strictly contemporary, the designation of masons in medieval building accounts, or fabric rolls, to use a term current among antiquaries. Mr. W. R. Lethaby's book "Westminster Abbey and the King's Craftsmen" (1906) gives us a good selection. We read of a "magister Robertus cementarius" in 1169 (p. 115). Then from the middle of the thirteenth century onwards we have a series of King's Masons beginning with Master John of Gloucester (p. 161, etc.) who are regularly called Master: but this was not merely an official title, for several other masons are so called, and in 1307 Master Richard de Wytham, mason (therefore already a master) was appointed to be Master at the King's Palace and the Tower, that is, director of the works. Towards the end of the thirteenth century timber was ordered "to make a lodge for Master Michael and his masons" (p. 181). "Master" therefore certainly meant something definite. Mr. Lethaby thinks there was some sort of gild which conferred the title, and mentions as a known fact that "in the fifteenth century there were yearly congregations of masters": of which more presently. The election by the masons of the City in 1315-6 of six paviors to repair the pavements (p. 186) proves that they were then recognized as an organized body.

There is also frequent mention of Master Carpenters, but nothing to show exactly how far their position was like that of Master Masons.

So far then we know that a master mason was a mason qualified in some ascertained way to undertake and control building operations, and that in the City of London there was an established community of masons in the early fourteenth century, probably much earlier. It does not seem likely that in such a body the designation of Master rested on nothing but unofficial reputation.

Riley's Memorials of London (1868) furnish valuable supplementary matter. In 1356 regulations were made for the trade of masons by "twelve of the most skilful men" equally representing the "masons hewers" and the "light masons and setters" (p. 280); these skilful men are referred to as "the said Masters so chosen" by the body of th trade. Among other rules "no one shall take work in gross" - that is as a contractor- "if he be not of ability in a proper manner to complete such work." In 1298 Master Simon de Pabingham and Master Richard de Wetham, masons, are reconciled before the Mayor (nature of difference not stated). As to Masters in other callings, the master farriers apparently control their trade (A.D. 1356, p. 292), and in the Barbers' gild it seems that the only Masters were the two elected Wardens (A.D. 1376, p. 394). Variations in the usage of different trades are only what we should expect.

Now let us turn to the Sacrist Rolls of Ely edited from the monuments of Ely Cathedral by Canon F.R. Chapman and dating from the late thirteenth and the first half of the fourteenth century. We meet with one John Attegrene who is mentioned several times during five years before he is entitled Magister Cementarius' in 1339-1840; therefore, in the learned editor's words, "not apparently at first a master mason, but attaining that distinction after some years": vol. i, p. 47; the words of the entry are "in stipend. Johannis Attegrene Magistri Cementarii per ann. 1.pound 6s. 8d" (ii. 99). Canon Chapman's inference appears not only natural but inevitable, and the supposition that "magister" was only a customary title of office during a particular employment is excluded by the evidence of the Westminster rolls already cited.

From the fabric rolls of York Minster published by the Surtees Society we learn that in the fourteenth century the regulations as to hours of work were laid down in detail by the Dean and Chapter, and the master masons and his fellows swore to observe them. The conditions on which a new worker is received are rather strict. After a week of probation the reception has to be "of the common assent of the master and keepers of the work, and of the master mason." The master and keepers first named appear to be supervisors appointed by the Dean and Chaper. If the master mason is disabled the warden ("magister secundarius cementariorum") is too act as deputy with half the salary."

It is certain that the trade had an active government of its own in the fourteenth century and that regular assemblies fixed or attempted to fix wages. "The masons seem to have resisted the Statutes of Labourers more successfully than any other craft." In 1360-1 (34 E. III, c. 9) Parliament declared all such trade regulations void as contrary to the Statute of Labourers (25 E. III. st. 2. c. 2, A. D. 1350) and insisted on wages being paid by the day and not otherwise according to the Statute at rates not exceeding 4d. a day for a "mestre mason de, franche peer" (freestone mason) and 3d. for others; but the right of lords to make their own bargains with contractors is saved. In 1425 (3 Hen. VI. c. 1. often cited in the modern literature of Freemasonry) this was reinforced by an absolute prohibition of the meetings themselves; the conveners were to be adjudged felons, and those attending to be liable to arbitrary fine and imprisonment. It is by no means clear that these Acts ever had much effect; in any case the Elizabethan lawyers treated them as repealed, though not expressly, by the legislation of their own time. All the medieval labor statutes were repealed in the course of the nineteenth century.

So far the extraneous evidence, as we may call it. As witness for the state of things about the end of the fourteenth century we have the operative masonic documents collectively known as Old Charges. A list of them is given in a most useful book to which we shall recur, Edward Conder's "Records of the hole craft and fellowship of masons," Lond. 1894, et. p. 219. The number there given as extant is 63, but in 1915 as many as 75 were known. Most of these are seventeenth century copies of earlier originals (one late 16th, about a dozen 18th), seemingly good copies in the main; but two, the "Halliwell" or "Regius" and the "Cooke," both in the British Museum, exist in actual medieval MSS, and moreover appear by internal evidence to be the earliest in original date. All these documents contain generally similar matter though not always in the same order; the usual order is as follows: (1) Invocation of the Trinity. (2) Definition of the liberal arts and especially geometry. (3) Origin of geometry and architecture given in a legendary chronicle form. The confusion of persons and times, such as Euclid being Abraham's clerk, and Charles Martel (in some MSS. corrupted into Marshall) speaking with a man who had been at the building of Solomon's temple, is no more than occurs in other medieval legends. (4) Foundation of masonry and yearly assemblies by King Athelstan." (5) Charges to be delivered to masons for their instruction: here the most considerable variations occur. There are "articles" addressed to masters and "points" to working fellows.

Let us now see what we can find about master masons in the Old Charges, beginning with the earliest.

The "Halliwell" or "Regius" document, the oldest of all in substance, is unique in its form, being versified. It is written in a "Gothic" hand of about the end of the fourteenth century; the text has been accessible in print for more than seventy years. The title is "constituciones artis gemetrie secundum Enclydem," geometry being identified with the higher skill of architecture (a word not yet known) as distinct from the mere journeyman's craft; and the space given to the relation of master and apprentice - an apprentice bound for seven years (v. 122) - is ample proof that the writer's object was quote practical. The apprentice must be free born, for otherwise his lord might reclaim him even in the lodge (v. 129 seq). The master is bound to teach the Prentice (v. 241); and the precept "to him that was higher in this degree" to "teach the simplest of wit" is exalted by being ascribed to Euclid (vv. 35-40). The prentice must keep his master's counsel's and what is done in the lodge to himself (vv. 275-286), but there is nothing to show whether any secrets are formally imparted to him or not; and every working mason is to take his pay from the master "full meekly" (v. 298).

Masters are the more skilful and worshipful of the craft (vv. 31-46) and are bound to attend general congregations of which they have notice, except for sickness or other reasonable excuse (vv. 105-118); evidently an important duty, as it has a whole "articulus" to itself. A master must not undertake work unless he is capable of carryings it through, as we have seen already (v. 195). Receipt of summonses to congregations would presumably be conclusive proof of mastership; whether there was any other form of admitting or recognizing masters does not appear so far. Masons (including masters, it would seem) address one another as fellows (v. 51). But at the assembly "there shall be masters and fellows also" (v. 409). If plain English words have any meaning, the writer regarded masters as superior to ordinary fellows, however their condition was acquired. These assemblies were public functions at which the Sheriff, the mayor of the city and other magnates were expected (v. 411). We cannot doubt that they were really held and did regulate the trade; otherwise there would have been no occasion for Parliament first to annul their rules and then to forbid them altogether.

Next we turn to the Cooke MS which need not be much later than the Regius; indeed the originals (for it is a combination of two documents, as Speth has proved in his excellent critical commentary appended to the Quatuor Coronatorum facsimile) may have been earlier. It is written in a book hand of the first half of the fifteenth century. The contents are in many ways peculiar. It begins with a sort of general thanks-giving instead of an invocation, and gives consecutively two different versions of the Euclidean legend, in the second of which the scribe mechanically copied the corrupt form "Englet" or "Englat." The first version refers (1. 640) to the "book of our charges," which probably resembled if it was not identical with the charges following the second version.

In a general way the matter is much like that of the Regius, but there is a unique passage about the congregations said to have been instituted in King Athelstan's time (1. 700 sqq.). These were to be annual or triennial, and "at such congregations they that be made masters should be examined of the articles after written, and be ransacked whether they be able and cunning to the profit of the lords" (i. e. employers) "of whom they take their pay for their service and for their travail," 1. 725. Evidently the author of this passage believed that a master mason's standing was not or ought not to be complete until he had satisfied the masters assembled in a regular congregation that he was well acquainted with the articles, that is, the duties of a master as delivered in the charges, and that he was competent as a practical undertaker of building works. The former branch of the examination may well have been on the way to become a mere ceremony at the beginning of the fifteenth century; we do not know how the latter was conducted, but perhaps testimonials of work actually accomplished would be accepted as sufficient proof of competence.

The later MS. recensions of constitutions and charges, read in their natural sense, plainly confirm the witness of the Regius and the Cooke MSS. that master and fellow were the names of distinct ranks. In an affirmative sentence, indeed, "masters and fellows" may be thought ambiguous. But there is nothing ambiguous about the repeated negative injunctions enumerating the various things that "no master nor fellow" or "no master nor no fellow" may do. Not that I assert or believe that the distinction was still alive when our present copies were written; but it must have been alive at the date of their originals. If "no master nor no fellow" is not a decisively disjunctive phrase, I do not know how the idea of two distinct classes is to be conveyed in the English language.

IV. THE FIFTEENTH CENTURY PRACTICE

What can we infer from our documents as to the actual usage of the later Middle Ages? I submit, with all due reserve and subject to correction or new information, that it was something like this. Any qualified fellow of the craft may take a contract if he can find an employer to intrust him with the work, and companions to work under him. So long as the building is in progress, be the time longer or shorter, he is "governor of the work" and called master, but strictly master only of the lodge he has formed for that special undertaking (there is no election of a master by the lodge in the purely operative period, except possibly, one may guess, if the master dies or is disabled before the work is finished). In order to obtain the permanent rank of Master he must be approved and certified in a general assembly. We have seen that the proceedings were public, and that public officers were present who were not members of the craft. It is therefore most improbable that any new secrets were then and there imparted to the approved master; indeed it is hard to see what more he can have had to learn.

Now let us turn again to the statement in the Cooke MS. about the examination of masters. It is not a common form; the author whose work our scribe copied must have made it with a purpose. It looks as if he thought the practice of examination had been unduly relaxed, and wished to reinforce it by the mythical authority of King Athelstan, or it may be that he objected to the methods of new unionism (to use a modern phrase) whereby the congregations fell foul of Parliament, and intended to give his companions a hint that it was better to stick to their ancient office of keeping up the technical standard. Again he may have had some personal interest in the fees paid by masters on approval and have been anxious about their falling off. Fees were a great matter in the Middle Ages. This, however, is guesswork.

Then the Cooke MS. has yet another curious passage after the "Points" - perhaps not in its right place, perhaps taken from a different source - where we hear of a class of "new men." "At the first beginning" (of the congregation) "new men that never were charged before be charged in this manner" - namely, in short, to keep no company with thieves, to work honestly, render true accounts in things for which they are accountable, behave as lawful men generally, "and that they keep with all their might and (sic) all the articles aforesaid:"

Something must be wrong with the text; for the duties specified are those of ordinary workers but the Articles dealt with those of masters. One suspects an accidental omission; perhaps we should read "[all the points] and all the articles aforesaid"; but the lacuna may be more considerable. We can infer, as the MS. stands, only that at these assemblies a charge in the nature of general exhortation and distinct from the "articles" and "points" was delivered to masters or fellows, or both, attending for the first time, and that every man newly qualified as fellow or master was bound to attend at the first opportunity. Charges of this type are familiar to all Brethren in our modern ritual. To my mind the passage (assuming it to be a correct statement of actual practice) leaves us in doubt whether this exhortation was the preface to a formal admission, and does not enable us either to affirm or to deny that there was such a ceremony.

On the while it seems likely that in the first half of the fifteenth century the craftsman who had executed one or two contracts with success was already apt to be so well content with the reputation of a de facto master as to be in no hurry to incur the trouble and expense of proceeding to the official completion of his title. But that completion may have been expected of a mason who aspired to be master of the works for a great undertaking such as the building of a collegiate church or material additions to a cathedral or minster. Similarly, in a rough way, the M. A. degree is kept alive in England at this day mainly as a qualification for academic franchise or scholastic or ecclesiastical office. The university analogy further suggests that only formally approved master masons had an effective vote in the general assemblies. I have not found any clear indication of the time when the practical business of the congregations died out, or when they ceased to be even formally convened; but I should guess that the former date cannot be put later than about the middle of the sixteenth, or the latter than the first quarter of the seventeenth century.

V. THE TRANSITION PERIOD

In the sixteenth century there was a general decay of the old craft regulations, those of masonry among them; but there was also a special reason for the standing of a master mason losing its importance. The introduction of the word "architect," hardly in use before the sixteenth and not common till the seventeenth century, marks the advent of a sort of men, trained not in the old craft ways, but in the new art that had come in with the new learning, who treated their profession as being of a higher order than the builder's industry. When the architect who had never been a craftsman was the real "governor of the work," and the master mason was no better than a foreman or clerk of the works, it was no longer worth while to be an operative master mason. The operative lodges gradually became little more than social clubs preserving the symbolic traditions of the craft with various degrees of care and fidelity, something like the Inns of Chancery in the legal profession when they ceased to be active bodies working in auxiliary subordination to the Inns of Court: and as a measure of self-preservation they reinforced themselves by adopting or "accepting" honorary members who had nothing to do with the operative craft. These "accepted" members were the ancestors of our modern fraternity, and "speculative" in the sense of having studied, or being deemed to have studied geometry and architecture without being craftsmen. We may see in the adoption of Sir Christopher Wren at the very latest stage of the transition, if it took place, an expiring attempt on behalf of the attenuated operative tradition to revive its credit by linking it with the new school of architecture. But the fact is in doubt; we have here an example of perhaps the most troublesome kind of minor historical problem, here the affirmative side rests on weak though in itself not incredible evidence, the negative on the lack of confirmation in the quarters where we might reasonably look for it. Aubrey's well known memorandum 1691 cannot, however, be dismissed as void of all foundation; no motive for invention appears, and if Wren was invited to become a brother late in his life, at is not unaccountable. The simplest explanation is that nobody thought of it sooner; or for some reason Wren may have had difficulties about accepting, and taken a long time to decide. A more careful diarist would have saved posterity much trouble by being at the small pains of ascertaining that the meeting he noted as appointed for that very day, May 18, 1691 was actually held. But Aubrey was careless. Later inaccurate gossip is of no value as confirmation, but so far as its particulars are inconsistent with Aubrey's contemporary note it is equally worthless as contradiction. As Chetwode Crowley judiciously said, Aubrey's testimony remains admissible for what it is worth. It seems just possible that Wren was adopted in expectation of active assistance, and that he failed to render it; if so there might be a grain of truth in Anderson's otherwise very suspicious story of his neglect. But, whether we decide for or against Sir Christopher's membership, or leave the matter as an unsolved puzzle, there is nothing in it to help us to any general conclusion.

We have anticipated a little, but the digression is not material. The really dark time of the transformation is the sixteenth century. Lodges had been temporary working associations for a time varying with the magnitude of the undertaking. They became local and permanent, with something of a superficial likeness to craft gilds, from which they were really as different as could be. There were, of course, real craft gilds of masons in the towns, distinguished from other trade gilds by the customary right of intercommoning, to borrow a legal term from another region, whereby the fellow of any one gild was entitled to be received and to work in the jurisdiction of any other. Hence the need of passwords and tokens for recognition. But we have no evidence that the fixing of lodges to a local habitation was accomplished by any process of amalgamation with gilds. That which actually happened in the singular case (so far as we know) of London was, as we shall immediately see, not so simple. It is easy to suppose then when a master mason of good repute had fulfilled a contract and had reason to expect another, his companions might find it more profitable to stay with him than to disperse in search of other work. That would account for a lodge acquiring a continuous existence, but it would bring it no nearer to the change of the master from the founder into an annually elected officer. I have not met with any light on the process, nor even any attempt to explain it. One little fact waiting to be fitted into its right place is that operative bodies continued to deliver the old charges, or abridgments of them, to their apprentices as late as the eighteenth century.

Early in the seventeenth century we have a glimpse of the transition from operative to speculative masonry nearly but not quite accomplished in the "new articles" that occur in a few MSS. of the constitutions. (34) No person is to be accepted a freemason "unless he shall have(?) a lodge of five freemasons at least, whereof one to be a master or warden" - where "master" is obviously the name of office only - "of that limit or division wherein such lodge shall be kept, and another of the trade of freemasonry." This is not altogether clear, but it seems that a lodge was not correctly formed without at least one operative member. Now the need for such a rule shows that in most lodges the majority had ceased to be operative. This was certainly the case, as we now know, in the Warrington Lodge to which Elias Ashmole was admitted in 1646; indeed it is at least doubtful whether any operative mason was present. "I was made a Free Mason" is the whole extent of Ashmole's disclosure as to what passed, besides the date and the names of members of the lodge attending. Many years later, in 1682, Ashmole attended a lodge "at Mason's Hall, London" where six named persons "were admitted into the Fellowship of Free Masons." Ashmole "was the Senior Fellow among them," and the Master of the Masons' Company (of London) is named among "the Fellows" present. There is no word of Ashmole having ever gone through any other ceremony than that of Oct. 16, 1646, at Warrington, or of any one being called Master except in virtue of his office for the time being. The natural inference is that an "accepted" i.e. non-operative freemason was admitted as a fellow without going even in form through the stage of an apprentice (though a cumulative ceremony is not absolutely negatived), and that there was no speculative degree corresponding to the old operative rank of master mason, which had become obsolete, or confounded with that of fellow, in the course of the sixteenth century; whether practice was uniform everywhere we cannot be quite sure, but at all events there is no sign of different usages in London, and at Warrington. Honorary degrees in universities are in like manner conferred without any mention at all of the stages passed through by an ordinary candidate, and indeed degrees are quite commonly so conferred by the governing body on office-holders if they are not already graduates of the university.

The Masons' Hall where Ashmole attended a lodge meeting was the hall of the Masons' Company of London, and the lodge was attached to the company in the sense that the company accepted honorary members through (and it seems only through) the lodge; but the company as a subsisting craft gild was more extensive than the lodge, and the records of the lodge, unfortunately not extant, were quite distinct from those of the company. This appears in the extracts from the Company's accounts, beginning in 1620, published by Bro. Conder. New members admitted to the Company and "coming on the livery upon acceptance of Masonry" paid distinct fees to the lodge and to the Company. Apprentices taking up their freedom in the regular way of the trade after serving their seven years under a freeman might and commonly did pay a special fee of 3s. 4d. for "admission then to be a Master." This had nothing to do with the lodge, for there is no corresponding item in the fees paid by the "accepted" members. It was therefore a survival of the old operative rank, consolidated with that of fellow - a rank still distinct from membership of any merely local body, even that of the eminent London Company, and carrying in theory the privilege of being free of the craft everywhere. Its working value however does not seem to have been rated high in the year 1636, judging by the amount of 3s. 4d. as compared with the 20s. paid "by way of gratuitie to this Companie." By rights, it would seem, the 3s. 4d. should have gone to some representative of the general assembly of masons and not into the Company's account. Evidently there had long ceased to be any such person; I may add by the way that I cannot believe there was a Grand Master of Freemasons (except so far as the president of a general assembly, so long as the assemblies were held, may be regarded as such for the occasion, as Speth suggests in his commentary on the Cooke MS.) or any regular body acting like a Grand Lodge, before 1717. The "admission to be a Master" still practised in the Masons' Company in 1636 appears to be the latest officially recorded trace of the use of that name in the old operative sense. An inventory of 1665 shows that the Company kept a list of "the names of the accepted Masons" - that is the members of the lodge - "in a fair inclosed frame with lock and key." Nothing in the Company's books tells us what became of that lodge. It may have died out or may have separated from the Company and continued under some new name; Bro. Conder suggests as a pious conjecture that the Lodge of Antiquity may have arisen from it.

The formation of purely speculative lodges not having any professed operative character appears to have begun only in the eighteenth century, not without discontent on the part of operative lodge members.

Finally we have Anderson's statement about the meeting of four lodges which was the origin of the Grand Lodge of England. "They and some old Brothers met at the said Apple-Tree, and having put into the Chair the oldest Master Mason (now the Master of a Lodge) they constituted themselves a Grand Lodge pro tempore in due form," etc. The same term is applied at little further on to the chairman of the assembly and feast held at the Goose and Gridiron on St. John the Baptist's day, 1717, when Sayer was elected Grand Master. It seems natural that an actual Master of a lodge should take the chair on both occasions. Anderson's phraseology may have been intended to minimize the fact that the only persons then recognized as master masons were those who were or had been Masters of lodges, Installed Masters as we now call them: but it does not appear to me that any certain inference can be drawn.

VI. THE SPECULATIVE RECONSTRUCTION

The state of things before the creation of the Grand Lodge of England seems to have been as follows:

In the community of operative masons there had been three grades, namely apprentice, fellow and master, resembling the undergraduate student, bachelor and master or doctor of a university.

The rank of master mason had become less important from the fifteenth century onwards. It was practically extinct about the middle of the seventeenth century.

In the subsisting lodges about 1700 there was only one rank, generally under the name of fellow, but it seems that an actual or past Master of a lodge was entitled to some precedence.

I have endeavoured to give a connected view of these stages, distinguishing those points which are established or made highly probable by good witness from those which are left open by the known evidence and give room for some latitude of conjecture. In my judgment no greater certainty is now to be looked for save by some unexpected stroke of good fortune.

The founders of modern freemasonry, having in their hands copies of the "Old Charges," and perhaps other material now lost, were acquainted with the old operative classification and proceeded to reconstruct it in the speculative form now familiar to us.

Thus was our stately and superb edifice, for so we may justly call it notwithstanding all confessed errors in design and faults of execution, built up on the ruins of the medieval order. Our founders were credulous their credulity, as too commonly happens, was not free from admixture of something indistinguishable from pious fraud; but the blemishes affect only details of their work. The last word must be of thankfulness for the daring ingenuity which rescued the permanent and cosmopolitan elements of the ancient craft symbolism and developed them with enhanced spiritual value.

IV. THE FIFTEENTH CENTURY PRACTICE

What can we infer from our documents as to the actual usage of the later Middle Ages? I submit, with all due reserve and subject to correction or new information, that it was something like this. Any qualified fellow of the craft may take a contract if he can find an employer to intrust him with the work and companions to work under him. So long as the building is in progress, be the time longer or shorter, he is "governor of the work" and called master, but strictly master only of the lodge he has formed for that special undertaking (there is no election of a master by the lodge in the purely operative period, except possibly, one may guess, if the master dies or is disabled before the work is finished). In order to obtain the permanent rank of Master he must be approved and certified in a general assembly. We have seen that the proceedings were public, and that public officers were present who were not members of the craft. It is therefore most improbable that any new secrets were then and there imparted to the approved master; indeed it is hard to see what more he can have had to learn.

Now let us turn again to the statement in the Cooke MS. about the examination of masters. It is not a common form; the author whose work our scribe copied must have made it with a purpose. It looks as if he thought the practice of examination had been unduly relaxed, and wished to reinforce it by the mythical authority of King Athelstan, or it may be that he objected to the methods of new unionism (to use a modern phrase) whereby the congregations fell foul of Parliament, and intended to give his companions a hint that it was better to stick to their ancient office of keeping up the technical standard. Again he may have had some personal interest in the fees paid by masters on approval and have been anxious about their falling off. Fees were a great matter in the Middle, Ages. This, however, is guesswork.

Then the Cooke MS. has yet another curious passage after the "Points" - perhaps not in its right place, perhaps taken from a different source - where we hear of a class of "new men." "At the first beginning" (of the congregation) "new men that never were charged before be charged in this manner" - namely, in short, to keep no company with thieves, to work honestly, render true accounts in things for which they are accountable, behave as lawful men generally, "and that they keep with all their might and (sic) all the articles aforesaid." Something must be wrong with the text; for the duties specified are those of ordinary workers, but the Articles dealt with those of masters. One suspects an accidental omission; perhaps we should read "[all the points] and all the articles aforesaid"; but the lacuna may be more considerable. We can infer, as the MS. stands, only that at these assemblies a charge in the nature of general exhortation and distinct from the "articles" and "points" was delivered to masters or fellows, or both, attending for the first time, and that every man newly qualified as fellow or master was bound to attend at the first opportunity. Charges of this type are familiar to all Brethren in our modern ritual. To my mind the passage (assuming it to be a correct statement of actual practice) leaves us in doubt whether this exhortation was the preface to a formal admission, and does not enable us either to affirm or to deny that there was such a ceremony.

On the whole it seems likely that in the first half of the fifteenth century the craftsman who had executed one or two contracts with success was already apt to be so well content with the reputation of a de facto master as to be in no hurry to incur the trouble and expense of proceeding to the official completion of his title. Put that completion may have been expected of a mason who aspired to be master of the works for a great undertaking such as the building of a collegiate church or material additions to a cathedral or minster. Similarly, in a rough way, the M.A. degree is kept alive in England at this day mainly as a qualification for academic franchise or scholastic or ecclesiastical office. The university analogy further suggests that only formally approved master masons had an effective vote in the general assemblies. I have not found any clear indication of the time when the practical business of the congregations died out, or when they ceased to be even formally convened; but I should guess that the former date cannot be put later than about the middle of the sixteenth, or the latter than the first quarter of the seventeenth century.

V. THE TRANSITION PERIOD

In the sixteenth century there was a general decay of the old craft regulations, those of Masonry among them; but there was also a special reason for the standing of a master mason losing its importance. The introduction of the word "architect," hardly in use before the sixteenth and not common till the seventeenth century, marks the advent of a sort of men, trained not in the old craft ways, but in the new art that had come in with the new learning, who treated their profession as being of a higher order than the builder's industry. When the architect who had never been a craftsman was the real "governor of the work," and the master mason was no better than a foreman or clerk of the works, it was no longer worthwhile to be an operative master mason. The operative lodges gradually became little more than social clubs preserving the symbolic traditions of the craft with various degrees of care and fidelity, something like the Inns of Chancery in the legal profession when they ceased to be active bodies working in auxiliary subordination to the Inns of Court; and as a measure of self-preservation they reinforced themselves by adopting or "accepting" honorary members who had nothing to do with the operative craft. These "accepted" members were the ancestors of our modern fraternity, and "speculative" in the sense of having studied, or being deemed to have studied, geometry and architecture without being craftsmen. We may see in the adoption of Sir Christopher Wren at the very latest stage of the transition, if it really took place, an expiring attempt on behalf of the attenuated operative tradition to revive its credit by linking it with the new school of architecture. But the fact is in doubt; we have here an example of perhaps the most troublesome kind of minor historical problem, where the affirmative side rests on weak though in itself not incredible evidence, the negative on the lack of confirmation in the quarters where we might reasonably look for it. Aubrey's well known memorandum of 1691 cannot, however, be dismissed as void of all foundation; no motive for invention appears, and if Wren was invited to become a brother late in his life, that is not unaccountable. The simplest explanation is that nobody thought of it sooner; or for some reason Wren may have had difficulties about accepting, and taken a long time to decide. A more careful diarist would have saved posterity much trouble by being at the small pains of ascertaining that the meeting he noted as appointed for that very day, May 18, 1691, was actually held. But Aubrey was careless. Later inaccurate gossip is of no value as confirmation, but so far as its particulars are inconsistent with Aubrey's contemporary note it is equally worthless as contradiction. As Chetwode Crawley judiciously said, Aubrey's testimony remains admissible for what it is worthy. It seems just possible that Wren was adopted in expectation of active assistance, and that he failed to render it; if so there might be a grain of truth in Anderson's otherwise very suspicious story of his neglect. But, whether we decide for or against Sir Christopher's membership, or leave the matter as an unsolved puzzle, there is nothing in it to help us to any general conclusion.

We have anticipated a little, but the digression is not material. The really dark time of the transformation is the sixteenth century. Lodges had been temporary working associations for a time varying with the magnitude of the undertaking. They became local and permanent, with something of a superficial likeness to craft gilds, from which they were really as different as could be. There were, of course, real craft gilds of masons in the towns, distinguished from other trade gilds by the customary right of intercommoning, to borrow a legal term from another region, whereby the fellow of any one gild was entitled to be received and to work in the jurisdiction of any other. Hence the need of passwords and tokens for recognition. But we have no evidence that the fixing of lodges to a local habitation was accomplished by any process of amalgamation with gilds. That which actually happened in the singular case (so far as we know) of London was, as we shall immediately see, not so simple. It is easy to suppose then when a master mason of good repute had fulfilled a contract and had reason to expect another, his companions might find it more profitable to stay with him than to disperse in search of other work. That would account for a lodge acquiring a continuous existence, but it would bring it no nearer to the change of the master from the founder into an annually elected officer. I have not met with any light on the process, nor even any attempt to explain it. One little fact waiting to be fitted into its right place is that operative bodies continued to deliver the old charges, or abridgments of them, to their apprentices as late as the eighteenth century.

Early in the seventeenth century we have a glimpse of the transition from operative to speculative Masonry nearly but not quite accomplished in the "new articles" that occur in a few MSS. of the constitutions. No person is to be accepted a Freemason "unless he shall have (?) a lodge of five Freemasons at least, whereof one to be a master or warden" - where "master" is obviously the name of office only - "of that limit or division wherein such Lodge shall be kept, and another of the trade of Freemasonry." This is not altogether clear, but it seems that a lodge was not correctly formed without at least one operative member. Now the need for such a rule shows that in most lodges the majority had ceased to be operative. This was certainly the case, as we now know, in the Warrington Lodge to which Elias Ashmole was admitted in 1646; indeed it is at least doubtful whether any operative mason was present. "I was made a Free Mason" is the whole extent of Ashmole's disclosure as to what passed, besides the date and the names of members of the lodge attending. Many years later, in 1682, Ashmole attended a lodge "at Mason's Hall, London" where six named persons "were admitted into the Fellowship of Free Masons." Ashmole "was the Senior Fellow among them," and the Master of the Masons' Company (of London) is named among "the Fellows" present. There is no word of Ashmole having ever gone through any other ceremony than that of Oct. 16, 1646, at Warrington, or of any one being called Master except in virtue of his office for the time being. The natural inference is that an "accepted," i.e. non-operative Free-mason was admitted as a fellow without going even in form through the stage of an apprentice (though a cumulative ceremony is not absolutely negatived), and that there was no speculative degree corresponding to the old operative rank of master mason, which had become obsolete, or confounded with that of fellow, in the course of the sixteenth century; whether practice was uniform everywhere we cannot be quite sure, but at all events there is no sign of different usages in London and at Warrington. Honorary degrees in universities are in like manner con-ferred without any mention at all of the stages passed through by an ordinary candidate, and indeed degrees are quite commonly so conferred by the governing body on officeholders if they are not already graduates of the university.

The Masons' Hall where Ashmole attended a lodge meeting was the hall of the Masons' Company of London, and the lodge was attached to the company in the sense that the company accepted honorary mem-bers through (and it seems only through) the lodge; but the company as a subsisting craft gild was more extensive than the lodge, and the records of the lodge, unfortunately not extant, were quite distinct from those of the company. This appears in the extracts from the Company's accounts, beginning in 1620, published by Bro. Conder. New members admitted to the Company and "coming on the livery upon acceptance of Masonry" paid distinct fees to the lodge and to the Company. Apprentices taking up their freedom in the regular way of the trade after serving their seven years under a freeman might and commonly did pay a special fee of 3s 4d for "admission then to be a Master." This had nothing to do with the lodge, for there is no corresponding item in the fees paid by the "ac-cepted'? members. It was therefore a survival of the old operative rank, consolidated with that of fellow - a rank still distinct from membership of any merely local body, even that of the eminent London Company, and carrying in theory the privilege of being free of the craft everywhere. Its working value, however, does not seem to have been rated high in the year 1636, judging by the amount of 3s. 4d. as compared with the 20s. paid "by way of gratuitie to this Companie." By rights, it would seem, the 3s. 4d. should have gone to some representative of the general assembly of masons and not into the Company's account. Evidently there had long ceased to be any such person. I may add by the way that I cannot believe there was a Grand Master of Freemasons (except so far as the president of a general assembly, so long as the assemblies were held, may be regarded as such for the occasion, as Speth suggests in his commentary on the Cooke MS.) or any regular body acting like a Grand Lodge, before 1717. The "admission to be a Master" still practiced in the Masons' Company in 1636 appears to be the latest officially recorded trace of the use of that name in the old operative sense. An inventory of 1665 shows that the Company kept a list of "the names of the accepted Masons" - that is the members of the lodge "in a fair inclosed frame with lock and key." Nothing in the Company's books tells us what became of that lodge. It may have died out or may have separated from the Company and continued under some new name; Bro. Conder suggests as a pious conjecture that the Lodge of Antiquity may have arisen from it.

The formation of purely speculative lodges not having any professed operative character appears to have begun only in the eighteenth century, not without discontent on the part of operative lodge members.

Finally we have Anderson's statement about the meeting of four lodges which was the origin of the Grand Lodge of England. "They and some old Brothers met at the said Apple-Tree, and having put into the Chair the oldest Master Mason (now the Master of a Lodge) they constituted themselves a Grand Lodge pro tempore in due form," etc. The same term is applied a little further on to the chairman of the assembly and feast held at the Goose and Gridiron on St. John the Baptist's day, 1717, when Sayer was elected Grand Master. It seems natural that an actual Master of a lodge should take the chair on both occasions. Anderson's phraseology may have been intended to minimize the fact that the only persons then recognized as master masons were those who were or had been Masters of lodges, Installed Masters as we now call them; but it does not appear to me that any certain inference can be drawn.

VI. THE SPECULATIVE RECONSTRUCTION

The state of things before the creation of the Grand Lodge of England seems to have been as follows:

In the community of operative masons there had been three grades, namely apprentice, fellow and master, resembling the undergraduate student, bachelor and master or doctor of a university.

The rank of master mason had become less important from the fifteenth century onwards. It was practically extinct about the middle of the seventeenth century.

In the subsisting lodges about 1700 there was only one rank, generally under the name of fellow, but it seems that an actual or past Master of a lodge was entitled to some precedence.

I have endeavoured to give a connected view of these stages, distinguishing those points which are established or made highly probable by good witness from those which are left open by the known evidence and give room for some latitude of conjecture. In my judgment no greater certainty is now to be looked for save by some unexpected stroke of good fortune.

The founders of modern Freemasonry, having in their hands copies of the "Old Charges," and perhaps other material now lost, were acquainted with the old operative classification and proceeded to reconstruct it in the speculative form now familiar to us.

Thus was our stately and superb edifice, for so we may justly call it notwithstanding all confessed errors in design and faults of execution, built up on the ruins of the medieval order. Our founders were credulous; their credulity, as too commonly happens, was not free from admixture of something indistinguishable from pious fraud; but the blemishes affect only details of their work. The last word must be of thankfulness for the daring ingenuity which rescued the permanent and cosmopolitan elements of the ancient craft symbolism and developed them with enhanced spiritual value.

The Royal Order of Scotland

Charles S. Lobingier

The Royal Order of Scotland occupies, in Scotch Masonry, a place corresponding to the Order of the Temple (Knights Templar) in the so-called York Rite of American Masonry. Each is the culminating order of its respective rite and each is open to those only who have received the degrees of symbolic lodge and chapter. Moreover, while their legends and symbolism differ widely, each is largely a Christian order.

Indeed the legend of the first degree (Heredom of Kilwinning) of the Royal Order, carries it back to the Culdees who introduced Christianity into Scotland; while the legend of its other degree (Rosy Cross) connects it with Robert Bruce and the gory field of Bannockburn where Masonic soldiers, who fought under that famous king, are alleged to have earned from him the reward of Knighthood in the form of this Order which they were privileged in their Grand Lodge to pass on to their successors.

The battle of Bannockburn was fought on June 24 (Summer St. John's Day), 1314, just a year after the widespread persecutions of the Templars had culminated in the tragic death, at the stake, of their last Grand Master, Jacques de Molai, "on a little island of the Seine" in Paris. There are other legends which connect these two events and which tell of Templars who fled from those persecutions to Scotland, joined the army of Robert Bruce and helped him to win his great victory.

Passing, however, to quote "our Masonic Thucy-dides" (1) .. . from fable to fact (and the Royal Order (2) has probably no more than its share, among the high grade orders, of fable) the tradition which connects it with the Masonry of France appears to have a basis of fact. For Gould traces the Royal Order to an English Provincial Grand Chapter existing before 1750 of which he says that "there can be little if any doubt that it was an echo of French Scots Masonry"; (3) while another learned authority (4) has expressed the opinion that the parent English Grand Chapter "was an offshoot of the Emperors' Rite of Perfection or Heredom."

CONNECTION WITH THE SCOTTISH RITE

As both of these phases of eighteenth-century French Masonry were forerunners (5) of the Ancient and Accepted Scottish Rite, it will be seen how close is the connection in origin between the latter and the Royal Order of Scotland. This is further illustrated by resemblances in the rituals, especially the phraseology, and it was doubtless that historic connection which attracted the great Masonic student, Albert Pike, and led him to establish the Royal Order of Scotland in the United States and to become its first Provincial Grand Master there. For the same reason the Scottish Rite student of today will find more of interest in these quaint and curious degrees (6) of the Royal Order, and is better equipped to understand and appreciate them, than the devotees of any other Rite. In the United States the Provincial Grand Masters following Albert Pike, have continued to be Scottish Rite dignitaries (7) and candidates are rarely if ever received into the Royal Order there who are not 32 degree Masons. The Provincial Grand Lodge of the United States assembles annually; in the odd years at the same time and place as the Supreme Council for the Southern Jurisdiction of the United States, and in the even years with that of the Northern Jurisdiction, thus keeping in close touch with the leaders of the Rite throughout the country. The degrees of the Royal Order are conferred only while a Supreme Council is in session, and the participants in the work, as well as the candidates, are active and usually prominent Scottish Rite Masons. But by the transplantation of the Royal Order to the Philippines the Scottish Rite Masons here who are eligible will have the opportunity of receiving its degrees at home - a privilege not enjoyed by their brethren of the United States.

EXPANSION

According to Gould (8) the Royal Order took root in Scotland after the middle of the eighteenth century. In legend and symbolry it is still Scotch and appeals no less strongly for that reason to thousands of American and other Masons whose ancestry harks back to the "bonnie braes" of Caledonia. (9) The King of Scotland is acclaimed as hereditary Grand Master (in succession to Robert Bruce) and at every Royal Order meeting a chair is kept vacant in the east for him. Traditionally, too, the Order was composed at first entirely of

Scotchmen and limited to sixty-three, (10) evidently as the product of the sacred numbers 9 and 7. But this, if anything more than tradition, did not long continue, for as early as 1786 a Provincial Grand Lodge was erected in France (11) which, within a quarter of a century, came to comprise twenty-six subordinate lodges and chapters, including two in the French colonies, two in Italy and one in Belgium. (12)

Other Provincial Grand Lodges have since been erected as follows:

Glasgow and West of Scotland	1859
New Brunswick, Nova Scotia, and Prince	
Edward Island	1863
The Open Ports of China and the Colony	
of Hong Kong	1865
Western India	1870
London and the Metropolitan Counties	1872
Lancashire and Cheshire	1874
Ontario and Quebec	1875
United States of America	1877
Aberdeenshire	1883
Natal	1885
Yorkshire	1886
Northumberland, Durham,	
and Cumberland	1893
Cape Colony	1893
Canton of Geneva	1893

In addition to the foregoing there are Provincial Grand Lodges of Hong Kong and South China and of the Straits Settlements while a Provincial Grand Lodge of the Philippines has just been constituted. Thus the Royal Order has spread to nearly every continent, encircling the globe and, from a national organization in a small country, has become more cosmopolitan, probably, than any other branch of Masonry except the Ancient and Accepted Scottish Rite. Like the premier Grand Lodge of England that of the Royal Order has its branches in many lands, but unlike the former the latter retains its direct connection and control as regards all the bodies which have emanated from it. As the Provincial Grand Master of the United States observed in his address at the dinner above referred to, the Grand Lodge of the

Royal Order is the only grand body of Great Britain which now exercises authority over a Masonic body in the United States. And this unique position enables it to establish and preserve a connection between Scotch Masonry and that of other countries. Nay more, in the Far East it is thus afforded a special opportunity, as the connecting link between the Scotch and American crafts, to use its good offices toward removing the unfortunate misunderstanding which has temporarily - let us hope no more- estranged the governing bodies of Capitular Masonry in the two countries.

That would be an achievement worth while and that alone would justify the extension of the Royal Order to the Philippines. But it is hoped also thereby to render available here those rewards for Masonic service which Bro. Fensch, in the article already quoted, mentions as being offered in certain other provinces. "Indeed," he says, "at the present time members of the Royal Order of Scotland in the British colonies of China and South Africa, and possibly some of the other Provincial Grand Lodges, are given the prestige and honors usually accorded to Masons of the 33 degree and highest degree of the Scottish Rite." But these provinces, he further says, it must be remembered, "restrict the membership to . . . those who have become distinguished in Masonic work in the Orient."

PROVINCIAL GRAND LODGE OF THE PHILIPPINES

The charter for a Provincial Grand Lodge of the Philippines was issued some time since but no action was taken thereunder until the writer had visited the United States and ascertained from Provincial Grand Master, George M. Moulton, of the Provincial Grand Lodge of the United States, that such a course would be agreeable to him. Both he and the other officers of that Grand Lodge manifested a broad and truly Masonic attitude in the matter, recognizing that it was entirely within the discretion of the Grand Lodge at Edinburgh and that, while the Philippines are American territory, their distance renders it more convenient and conducive to the welfare of the order to establish a Provincial Grand Lodge there.

Such a generous attitude having removed all obstacles the event was auspiciously consummated on the evening of March 15, 1920, at the new Masonic Temple in Manila. The two degrees of Heredom of Kilwinning and Rosy Cross were conferred in full, and in the interval between them the company repaired to one of Manila's famous restaurants, near by, where a substantial repast, marked by much good fellowship, was partaken of.

The charter was then read and the newly obligated members requested to express their choice for officers by formal ballot. The charter left their selection to the Provincial Grand Master but it was deemed better for the new body, and more calculated to start it with enthusiasm, to invite a formal expression from the members. The balloting was accompanied by much good feeling, and the officers chosen include some of the most active and prominent members of the Craft in the Philippines. Thus the Deputy Grand Master is a 33 degree Mason and is now Junior Grand Warden of the symbolic Grand Lodge of the Philippines of which body also the new Provincial Senior Grand Warden of the Royal Order is a Past Grand Master and at present, Grand Secretary. The roster of officers below Provincial Grand Master is as follows:

Frederic H. Stevens, Provincial Dep. Grand Master. Newton C. Comfort, Provincial Grand Sen. Warden. J. Frank Brown, Provincial Grand Junior Warden. Warren W. Weston, Provincial Grand Secretary. Aziz T. Hashin, Provincial Grand Treasurer Eugene A. Perkins, Provincial Grand Chaplain. Victor Hall, Provincial Grand Sword Bearer. Amos D. Haskell, Provincial Grand Banner Bearer. John J. Riehl, Provincial Grand Steward Frank Towle, Provincial Grand Steward. Elmer Jeen, Provincial Grand Guarder.

After the ballots had been taken the principal officers were, installed and formal proclamation was made that the Provincial Grand Lodge of the Philippines had now been constituted. Some business was then transacted, not the least important of which was the unanimous adoption of a resolution of thanks to M.'. W.'. James H. Osborne, Past Provincial Grand Master for the open ports of China, whose friendly and fraternal interest in the new Philippine body was one of the strong factors in securing its charter.

Profoundly appreciated also, was the Resolution recommended by Provincial Grand Master Moulton and adopted by the Provincial Grand Lodge of the United States as follows:

"Resolved, that the Provincial Grand Lodge of the Royal Order of Scotland for the United States of America heartily approves of the action of the Grand Lodge at Edinburgh for the formation of a Provincial Grand Lodge of the R.O.S. to be located at Manila in the

Philippine Islands, and the appointment of Bro. Charles Sumner Lobingier to be the first Provincial Grand Master thereof.

"We hail the addition of this new offspring to our parent body with great joy, and extend to it a most cordial welcome into fraternal relations, expressing for its membership, now and hereafter, our earnest wishes for the perpetuity and prosperity of their undertaking, and the fervent hope that its good works may be in evidence until the end of time."

The "Ides of March" will long be remembered as red letter day in the annals of the old Royal Order in new field.

NOTES:

(1) Gould, *History of Freemasonry, III*, 75.

(2) Woodford (*Cyclopedia of Freemasonry*, 586), (1878), was "quite prepared to concede it a considerable antiquity as a high grade."

(3) *History of Freemasonry, III*, 76. On page 92 of the same volume he says: "It cannot be too strongly insisted upon, that all so-called Scottish Masonry has nothing whatever to do with the Grand Lodge of Scotland, nor, with one possible exception - that of the Royal Order of Scotland - did it ever originate in that country. If we add to this rite that of the Ancient and Accepted Scottish Rite of 33 degree, we may even maintain that none of the Scots degrees were at any time practised in Scotland. As a slight mark of distinction I shall therefore, whenever possible, allude to these degrees as Scots and not Scottish."

(4) Allgemaines Handbuch der Freimaurerei, (Leipsic, 1863-79) s.v. Heredom.

(5) Gould, *History of Freemasonry, III*, 92, 93, 129.

(6) One of the attractive features is that the Ritual is partly in rhyme.

(7) The present Provincial Grand Master in the United States is Bro. George M. Moulton, 33 degree, who is also an Honorary Member of the Supreme Council of the Northern Jurisdiction as well as prominent in all other branches of Masonry.

(8) *History of Freemasonry, III*, 76.

(9) At the annual dinner of the Royal Order which it was the writer's privilege to attend in Washington, Oct. 16, 1917, Scotch dishes were served, Scotch airs played, (partly with a bagpipe), the program

cover design included a thistle, and one of the speakers was a Scratch General, lately from Flanders fields.

(10) Bro. Albert Fensch, formerly of the Philippines, and who received the degrees of the Royal Order in Hong Kong, wrote an article on the subject for the Texas Freemason (reprinted in the American Tyler-Keystone for September, 1915) in which he said: "The Provincial Grand Lodges of Hongkong, South China and Straits settlements still restrict the membership to sixty-three and they of those who have become distinguished in Masonic work in the Orient."

(11) Gould, *History of Freemasonry, III*, 76, 161.

(12) Thory, *Annales Originis*, 173.

The Square and the Cross
A.S. MacBride

Masons, generally, do not associate the square with the cross; yet essentially they are the same. The cross is composed of right angles, or squares. It is found on rocks chiselled in the prehistoric ages and in graves carved on rude pottery buried with bodies whose very bones in the course of thousands of years have crumbled into dust, and on the top of which lie the ruins of periods and of peoples of whom history has not the faintest trace. It is found thus, not in an isolated spot, but in regions scattered far apart. It is the most universal of all symbols. In the Hindu temples, in the Egyptian pyramids, in the ruined altars of America, and in the churches of Christendom, ancient and modern alike, it occupies a conspicuous position.

The cross — with a circle round it — is associated with the earliest known relics of humanity, with the most ancient carvings and records of India, and with coins and medals belonging to a pre-Christian age in France and elsewhere.

In all kinds the cross is formed of right angles, and the circle is implied where not shown. In the Latin and Greek forms generally the circle has disappeared, but it is still found at times, particularly in paintings, where it is shown as a halo of light behind the cross. As the craftsman in making the cross has first to form the circle and from its center work out the limbs, the circle must always be assumed to be present, even where it does not appear. The oldest form always has the circle. In the Egyptian form, the circle is placed on the top, and the vertical limb is lengthened, evidently to form a handle. To the Egyptians this circle symbolized the generative, or productive power, in nature. It is the transverse section of the egg, which was also used sometimes in its upright shape, in the form of a loop or oval. We find the Hindus representing the same idea, also by a loop, but in every case the circle, or loop, is associated with the cross. The basis of Gothic architecture is the cross, the triangle and the loop, all of which are inter-related. The cross and triangle form the base of the plan, and the loop forms the plan for the windows, doors, and sometimes the roof.

Laying aside details not helpful to our present purpose, let us turn our attention to the general ideas connected with this symbol.

The ancients of Asia, Africa and Europe considered the circle as the symbol of the Divine One circumscribing Himself, so as to become manifested to us. The limitations of human nature demand this restriction, for, otherwise, we could have no knowledge of Him. Without the limiting circle we gaze on boundless space, incomprehensible and void of any idea to our minds. We must have form before we can have ideas. The blank page of a book conveys nothing. Draw on it a flower, or an animal, and an idea is presented to the mind. Thus, the Divine One circumscribed Himself in His Creation and for our sakes clothed Himself in a garment of matter, so that he might be manifested to us. The material universe is everywhere a circumscribing of the Infinite and the cross symbolizes the Divine manifestations of Power, Light, Life and Love.

The first Divine manifestation symbolized-by the cross is that of Power. The two lines of the cross, intersecting at right angles in the center and extending to the utmost limits of the circle, represent the two great central forces which dominate all matter and which we have already considered in the law of the square in nature. If we work with these forces the Divine Power in them will manifest itself by working with us. If we work against them, it will manifest itself by destroying our work. They work on the square . . . and we must therefore work on the square if we are to have the Divine Power with us.

The second Divine manifestation symbolized by the cross is that of Light. Darkness is infinite and expresses nothing. Light is circumscribed that it may be manifested. It comes out of darkness and is lost in darkness. The energy from the sun comes to our earth through the boundless ether: cold, silent, and in darkness. Did it come in the form of direct Light the whole heavens would be a blaze and we would see nothing else. Not until it impinges on our atmosphere does it burst into light. In the same way, electricity is unseen in the wire until it meets with the resisting carbon. Coal-gas, the common candle, and the lamp, are all enveloped in darkness until they manifest their light in almost essentially similar, although apparently, different conditions. In all these varied conditions, however, light manifests itself on the square. The energy from the sun strikes our atmosphere at right angles and bursts into light. A rope, stretched out with one end fastened and the other end shaken by the hand, appears to have waves running from end to end. In reality it is moving up and down, at right angles to the line of progress. Science tells us it is in this way light moves. It works on the square, and the circle with the square, or cross, is a fitting symbol of the manifestation of material light.

But this symbol is particularly representative of moral light. That only can be light morally that is true and square. Beliefs and doctrines that do not accord with the right angle of our conscientious convictions, can never give light.

The third Divine manifestation symbolized by the cross is that of Life. Through all nature there are two great elemental principles variously called the active and the passive, the positive and the negative, the male and the female. The various units of atoms, molecules, vegetables and animals possess one, or both, of these principles. In the inanimate kingdom, the term "polarity" and "affinity" are employed to indicate the action of these principles and the relation of the one to the other. In the animate kingdom the word "sex" is used for the same purpose. In both kingdoms everywhere we find these two elemental principles at work. The formation of a crystal and of a crystaloid, the building of a tree and of a man, all seem to proceed along the lines of two main forces working at right angles—that is, working on the square. The atoms, which form the basis of the material creation, have their positive and negative poles. According to the latest scientific discoveries, they are the product of electricity and something called protyle, the one being active and the other passive.

But it is for the spiritual truths which this symbol reveals and yet conceals that it is of greatest importance to us. In the frescoes of the pyramids we see it in the hands of the god, as the symbol of regeneration. The dead one is shown lying on the ground in the form of a mummy, and the god is coming to touch his lips with it and revivify his body. Ages before Egyptian civilization dawned, it was carved on pottery, and buried with human bodies along with food and weapons, the evidence, even in that early period, of a faith in a resurrection and a life beyond the tomb.

It is a somewhat saddening and peculiar fact that this sacred symbol should have been associated with, what appears to us to be, a vile and most degrading worship. While the phallic cult may have originally been the recognition of a Divine purpose running through all the arrangements for the propagation of life, and of the symbolic lesson therein of a spiritual regeneration, yet the broad fact remains that the multitude saw in it the reflex of their own animal passions. It brought ruin on the Greek and Roman empires. Had the glory of art, the abundance of wealth, the grandeur of philosophy, or the culture of the intellect, possessed any power of salvation, these peoples would have survived. But salvation is neither possible to the individual nor to the community that is impure. If you worship the brute, a brute you will be. If you would be divine, worship the Divine.

The fourth Divine manifestation symbolized by the cross is that of Love. From the degrading associations of phallic worship this symbol had to be purged and purified by blood and sorrow. For many years it was an instrument of tyranny for the infliction of cruel and intense suffering. There can be little doubt but thousands suffered on it whose only fault was in being too good to be understood. The divine soul everywhere is at first misunderstood. His language is heaven-born and his earth-bound hearers cannot interpret it. Hence the thorny crown of derision. The good are not allowed to pursue their quiet path. They are dragged into the full blaze of fame and their pains and punishment become their glory. Love's best work is most likely to be rejected and despised. . . . Suffering is the perfecting process of the perfect ashlar. Insensibility is the sign of degradation. Capacity for suffering is the mark and insignia of rank in the scale of evolution. The higher the love, the deeper the sorrow. Through tribulation the higher forms of life are born.

When is a Man a Mason?

Joseph Fort Newton

When he can look out over the rivers, the hills, and the far horizon with a profound sense of his own littleness in the vast scheme of things, and yet have faith, hope, and courage-which is the root of every virtue.

When he knows that down in his heart every man is as noble, as vile, as divine, as diabolic, and as lonely as himself, and seeks to know, to forgive, and to love his fellowman.

When he knows how to sympathize with men in their sorrows, yea, even in their sins-knowing that each man fights a hard fight against many odds.

When he has learned how to make friends and to keep them, and above all how to keep friends with himself.

When he loves flowers, can hunt birds without a gun, and feels the thrill of an old forgotten joy when he hears the laugh of a little child.

When he can be happy and high-minded amid the meaner drudgeries of life.

When star-crowned trees and the glint of sunlight on flowing waters subdue him like the thought of one much loved and long dead.

When no voice of distress reaches his ears i vain, and no hand seeks his aid without response.

When he finds good in every faith that helps any man to lay hold of divine things and sees majestic meanings in life, whatever the name of that faith may be.

When he can look into a wayside puddle and see something beyond mud, and into the face of the most forlorn fellow mortal and
see something beyond sin.
When he knows how to pray, how to love, how to hope.

When he has kept faith with himself, with his fellowman, and with
his God; in his hands a sword for evil, in his heart a bit of a song-
glad to live, but not afraid to die!

Such a man has found the only real secret of Masonry, and the one
which it is trying to give to all the world.

More Masonic Books from Cornerstone

The Three Distinct Knocks
by Samuel Pritchard
6x9 Softcover 100 pages
ISBN 1613421826

Jachin and Boaz
by Samuel Pritchard
6x9 Softcover 92 pages
ISBN 1613421834

An Encyclopedia of Freemasonry
by Albert Mackey
Revised by William J. Hughan and Edward L. Hawkins
Foreword by Michael R. Poll
8.5 x 11, Softcover 2 Volumes 960 pages
ISBN 1613422520

Outline of the Rise and Progress of Freemasonry in Louisiana
by James B. Scot
Introduction by Alain Bernheim
Afterword by Michael R. Poll
8x10 Softcover 180 pages
ISBN 1-934935-31-X

In His Own (w)Rite
by Michael R. Poll
6×9 Softcover 176 pages
ISBN: 1613421575

Seeking Light
The Esoteric Heart of Freemasonry
by Michael R. Poll
6×9 Softcover 156 pages
ISBN: 1613422571

Cornerstone Book Publishers
www.cornerstonepublishers.com

More Masonic Books from Cornerstone

Masonic Enlightenment
The Philosophy, History and Wisdom of Freemasonry
Edited by Michael R. Poll
6 x 9 Softcover 180 pages
ISBN 1-887560-75-0

Morgan: The Scandal That Shook Freemasonry
by Stephen Dafoe
Foreword by Arturo de Hoyos
6x9 Softcover 484 pages
ISBN 1-934935-54-9

Masonic Questions and Answers
by Paul M. Bessel
6 x 9 Softcover 144 pages
ISBN 1-887560-59-9

Our Stations and Places - Masonic Officer's Handbook
by Henry G. Meacham
Revised by Michael R. Poll
6 x 9 Softcover 164 pages
ISBN: 1-887560-63-7

Knights & Freemasons: The Birth of Modern Freemasonry
By Albert Pike & Albert Mackey
Edited by Michael R. Poll
Foreword by S. Brent Morris
6 x 9 Softcover 178 pages
ISBN 1-887560-66-1

Robert's Rules of Order: Masonic Edition
Revised by Michael R. Poll
6 x 9 Softcover 212 pages
ISBN 1-887560-07-6

Cornerstone Book Publishers
www.cornerstonepublishers.com

More Masonic Books from Cornerstone

The Freemasons Key
A Study of Masonic Symbolism
Edited by Michael R. Poll
6 x 9 Softcover 244 pages
ISBN: 1-887560-97-1

**The Ancient and Accepted Scottish Rite
in Thirty-Three Degrees**
by Robert B. Folger
Introduction by Michael R. Poll
ISBN: 1-934935-88-3

The Bonseigneur Rituals
Edited by Gerry L. Prinsen
Foreword by Michael R. Poll
8x10 Softcover 2 volumes 574 pages
ISBN 1-934935-34-4

A.E. Waite: Words From a Masonic Mystic
Edited by Michael R. Poll
Foreword by Joseph Fort Newton
6 x 9 Softcover 168 pages
ISBN: 1-887560-73-4

Freemasons and Rosicrucians - the Enlightened
by Manly P. Hall
Edited by Michael R. Poll
6 x 9 Softcover 152 pages
ISBN: 1-887560-58-0

Masonic Words and Phrases
Edited by Michael R. Poll
6 x 9 Softcover 116 pages
ISBN: 1-887560-11-4

Cornerstone Book Publishers
www.cornerstonepublishers.com

www.ingramcontent.com/pod-product-compliance
Lightning Source LLC
Chambersburg PA
CBHW021058090426
42738CB00006B/396